THE UNOFFICIAL

STRANGER
THINGS
A-Z

THE UNOFFICIAL

STRANGER THINGS A-Z

DANIEL BETTRIDGE

JOHN BLAKE

Published by John Blake Publishing Ltd,
3 Bramber Court, 2 Bramber Road,
London W14 9PB, England

www.johnblakebooks.com

www.facebook.com/johnblakebooks
www.twitter.com/jblakebooks

This edition published in 2017

ISBN: 978 1 78606 470 7

British Library Cataloguing–in–Publication Data:

A catalogue record for this book is available from the British Library.

Design by www.envydesign.co.uk

Printed in Great Britain by CPI Group (UK) Ltd

1 3 5 7 9 10 8 6 4 2

Papers used by John Blake Publishing are natural, recyclable products made from
wood grown in sustainable forests. The manufacturing processes conform to the
environmental regulations of the country of origin.

Every attempt has been made to contact the relevant copyright–holders,
but some were unobtainable. We would be grateful if the appropriate people
could contact us.

John Blake Publishing is an imprint of Bonnier Publishing
www.bonnierpublishing.com

AUTHOR BIOGRAPHY

Daniel Bettridge is a journalist, author and pop culture junkie who has written for some of the world's leading publications including *The Guardian*, *The Independent*, *The Atlantic*, Vulture, *Total Film*, *Radio Times*, and *The Times*. He is also the author of *The Travel Guide to the Seven Kingdoms of Westeros*, a fictional guide for *Game of Thrones* fans.

A

ACROBAT THEORY

Featured in the fifth episode of the show's first season 'The Flea and the Acrobat', the Acrobat theory is an analogy posited by science teacher extraordinaire Mr Clarke to explain travel between multiple dimensions. Mr Clarke puts forward his analogy after being confronted by the boys at Will Byers' wake.

Mr Clarke's analogy asks the boys to picture their own dimension as a tightrope, and all of the people living on it as acrobats. The tightrope has rules. To the acrobat the tightrope is flat, they can walk forwards and backwards along it but that's it. They can't go upside down. The teacher then asks the boys to imagine a flea standing next to the acrobat. The flea can go forwards and backwards along the rope just like his precariously perched partner, but it can also travel along the sides of the rope or underneath of it. The flea isn't limited and so can travel to dimensions that the acrobat can't.

Mr Clarke's theory is accompanied by a sketch drawing on a conveniently discarded paper plate, a scientific scribble that has subsequently become one of the most endearing images of the series, recreated on everything from t-shirts to posters. The paper plate also serves as a handy tool to show how you could travel between the dimensions, munching a hole through the plate to show how a rift could create a gateway. As it turns out the moustachioed mentor's hastily scribbled analogy actually has a basis in reality, and can be compared to a similar idea put forward by renowned string theorist Professor Brian Greene. In a 2008 speech on string theory Greene put forward his own analogy involving an ant on a powerline.

'So, imagine you're looking at something like a cable supporting a traffic light', Professor Greene explained. 'It's in Manhattan. You're in Central Park – it's kind of irrelevant – but the cable looks one-dimensional from a distant viewpoint, but you and I all know that it does have some thickness. It's very hard to see it, though, from far away. But if we zoom in and take the perspective of, say, a little ant walking around – little ants are so small that they can access all of the dimensions – the long dimension, but also this clockwise, counter-clockwise direction … this illustrates the fact that dimensions can *be of two sorts: big and small. And the idea that maybe the big dimensions around us are the ones that we can easily see, but there might be additional dimensions curled up, sort of like the circular part of that cable, so small that they have so far remained invisible.'*

So how scientifically accurate is Mr Clarke's theory? It does a nice job of explaining the multiple dimensions proposed by string theory. However the Upside Down place itself undoes the science a little as the extra dimensions proposed by string theorists are tiny, and only accessible by minute particles, not terrifying monsters and hapless middle school students.

AFTER SHOW

Following on from the trend established by hit shows such as *The Walking Dead* and *Game of Thrones*, Netflix decided to jump on the After Show bandwagon with *Stranger Things*. The imaginatively titled *Stranger Things After Show* is the streaming service's first official aftershow and an interesting development in the company's continued plans to bring viewers fresh original content. Hosted by DJ Jesse Janedy, alongside Tiona Hobson, Roxy Striar, and Zach Wilson the show was made available via Netflix's YouTube channel and attracted more than 100,000 views per episode. It was also made available as a free podcast on iTunes.

ALIEN (1979) / *ALIENS* (1986)

There is no shortage of references to the silver screen sprinkled across *Stranger Things*, with the Duffer Brothers deliberately including hat tips towards some of their favourite films. One clear influence on them is the *Alien* sci-fi movie franchise, which began with Ridley Scott's chest-poppingly popular first instalment from 1979, which helped to set the tone for the genre for generations to come.

Whilst there are no direct references to the film in the series, the franchise's infamous Xenomorphs have clearly been an influence on the Demogorgon creature, most notably in the sticky residue it leaves in its wake as well as its use of humans as live incubators.

ATARI

The dream Christmas present of choice for the boys of Hawkins, Indiana in 1983 seems to be the Atari 2600. Will got one, Dustin got one and probably every kid who made it to Santa's nice list in the early 1980s got one. The Atari was the bleeding edge games console of the decade – a wood veneered masterpiece that has sold more than 30 million units since its original release in 1977, which was famous for games such as Pong, Adventure and Pitfall.

The inclusion of Atari in the series has also spawned an entire subgenre of fan art, with dedicated viewers creating everything from *Stranger Things* Atari cartridges to posters and even graphics of what an Atari game based on the show might look like.

AUDITIONS

It's hard to imagine *Stranger Things* without its current cast but the audition process for the series was tough, really tough. In total 906 boys and 307 girls were screened in order to find the most suitable leads. 'We knew this would be impossible without the right ensemble of actors,' the Duffer Brothers told *Entertainment Weekly*. 'Casting is always a challenge, even more so on a show where four of the leads are 12 years old. A cringeworthy child performance will kill a movie or show like almost nothing else. We've found that the key to finding good kid actors is actually rather obvious: You just have to audition pretty much every kid in the world who wants to act.'

The search might have been exhaustive but the process was equally in-depth. Alongside select scenes from the series' script, the Duffer Brothers also had the children read scenes from the 1986 coming-of-age classic *Stand By Me*. The movie is a clear influence on the finished show and one which the Duffer Brothers have repeatedly referenced as one of their favourite films. Finally after creating a shortlist from more than 1,000 hopefuls the casting team flew all of the kids out to LA in order to watch them audition together in order to test their chemistry. This involved bringing the child actors together from locations as far away as New York, Canada and the UK.

To help them find the right talent, the Duffer Brothers turned to Emmy Award-winning Casting Director Carmen Cuba. Cuba has worked with some of the biggest names in the business including Steven Soderbergh, Ridley Scott and Oliver Stone. She has become one of Hollywood's key professionals, working on hit movies such as *The Martian*, *Magic Mike XXL*, and *Now You See Me*, alongside TV shows such as *Narcos*, *Sense8*, and *The Girlfriend Experience*.

Speaking to *Backstage* magazine Cuba revealed that casting the young actors was one of her favourite parts of the process. 'This was the first time I was casting actors who were in the same age range as my two sons, and I realize now that this was a big factor for who I gravitated to in these roles. Being able to experience the young actors with this very present sense of what, at that age, a person is like, how deeply they think and feel, how connected they are to their younger selves, and yet how fragile they are while transitioning into that next independent phase, was special for me. It might sound corny, but my connection to my own children at this magical time in their lives informed the qualities I wanted these kids to have as people and as actors.'

One of the key successes in *Stranger Things* is that the production team didn't just cast great actors, but great child actors. It's easy to imagine how much worse the result might have been had they attempted to cast recognizable faces for the leading roles, or followed *The OC* / *Beverly Hills 90210* formula by casting older actors for younger roles. It's also refreshing to see a show that casts kids that are altogether more real than the impossibly perfect pre-teens rolled out in Disney's television output. These aren't aspiring models or wannabe pop stars, they are real kids with real personalities, something that helps to make the *Stranger Things* squad all the more endearing.

It's not only the child actors who make *Stranger Things* – it's also the grown-up stars. Winona Ryder was by far the stand out name in amongst the eclectic cast list. The actress was apparently first choice to play the role of Joyce. 'We grew up in the early '90s, so we were very well acquainted with Winona's films,' the Duffer Brothers told *Entertainment Weekly*. 'We loved the idea of seeing Winona back on screen in a leading role. As fans, we just really missed her, and we believed that a lot of other people felt the same way. So we sent her the script and crossed our fingers...'

Casting for the second season of the show began the same day that Netflix announced they would be renewing the series. In total three new recurring characters were being sought to join the residents of Hawkins for *Stranger Things*' sophomore outing.

AV CLUB

In keeping with their nerd personas the boys in *Stranger Things* are all members of Hawkins Middle School A.V. Club. For those not in the know, A.V. Club is short for audiovisual club. At American schools these clubs were formed of technically minded students who were in charge of maintaining and managing audio visual equipment including radios, PAs and film projectors.

Hawkins Middle School's A.V. Club, run by Mr Clarke, gives its young members access to a newly purchased Heathkit Ham Radio. First introduced in the opening episode the boys' excitement is summed up by Lucas: 'When Will sees this he's totally gonna blow his shit!' The radio eventually acts as the medium through which the boys contact Will in the Upside Down dimension. Using Eleven's abilities, which she earlier demonstrates with the crew's walkie-talkies, the boys fry the radio set up, but not before getting a faint signal that proves that Will is still alive.

Heathkits were the name given to electronic equipment that was sold to hobbyists and educational institutions by the Heath Company. Operating from 1947 to 2012 the Heath Company was renowned for its amateur radio equipment. These affordable and easy-to-understand rigs were hugely popular with enthusiasts and would have been an exciting addition to any geek's life in the 1980s when *Stranger Things* is set.

B

B&Q

The series' popularity with fans had an unexpected impact on British DIY giant B&Q. Leading up to Christmas 2016 the company revealed that, as a result of *Stranger Things* mania, it was struggling to keep up with demand for LED lights. Some stores revealed that their shelves were entirely emptied of lights thanks to the role they play in the show, and the chain confirmed that sales had rocketed.

In a statement B&Q's market director for Christmas, Mike Norton, said: 'The popularity of *Stranger Things* has had a completely unexpected effect on the sale of our multicolour Christmas string lights this year. We've seen a huge spike in demand and the lights are by far our bestselling range thanks to the show's huge following.'

The DIY chain was clearly enjoying the unexpected sales boom as a result of the show. Norton joked: 'Despite the similarity in the lights, we'd like to remind customers that this product should not be used to try to contact the "upside down". B&Q cannot claim any responsibility for Demogorgon-related damage to homes this Christmas.'

BANDANA

It was actor Caleb McLaughlin who suggested adding an eye-catching element to his character Lucas's costume. Sure enough, towards the end of *Stranger Things*' first season, Lucas began to wear a camouflage bandana.

'THE BATHTUB'

'The Bathtub' was the name given to Chapter 7 of the show's first season. It was written by John Doble and directed by the Duffer Brothers. The episode takes its name from the sensory deprivation tank that is used to enhance Eleven's powers.

Through flashbacks we see an advanced version of the sensory deprivation tank at Hawkins Laboratory as Eleven is tasked first with spying on a Russian agent and subsequently with contacting the Monster she encounters in the Upside Down. Later in the series the show's heroes create a makeshift sensory deprivation tank at Hawkins Middle School using a paddling pool, some de-icing salt, and the scientific know-how of Mr Clarke who informs the boys they'd need 1,500lbs of salt to create their makeshift isolation tank. The heroes use the tank to amplify Eleven's abilities, enabling her to locate Barb's body as well as Will's hiding place.

Eleven isn't the only person to have used a sensory deprivation tank on *Stranger Things*. Becky Ives, Terry's sister, tells Joyce Byers and Chief Hopper that, as part of government experiments, Terry would be stripped naked and placed in sensory deprivation tanks whilst using psychedelic drugs. The description of the MKUltra processes is actually close to real life experiments. In 1973 for example a team of parapsychologists, led by senior research associate Charles Honorton, was given a $52,000 grant from the US Government to use sensory deprivation tanks in an attempt to prove the existence of ESP (extra-sensory perception). Today, sensory deprivation tanks, known as Floatation tanks, are a common form of spa treatment, used to promote relaxation.

BENNY'S BURGERS

Located at 4819 Randolph Lane in Hawkins, Indiana, Benny's Burgers is a fictional diner that appears in the opening two episodes of *Stranger Things*' first season. Owned and run by Benny Hammond (played by Chris Sullivan) we're told that the family-run business has been cooking up a storm in the sleepy town since 1956.

We're first given a glimpse of the diner in the opening

episode when a hospital gown clad Eleven breaks in and starts stealing fries. After catching the young runaway in the act, Benny takes it upon himself to clothe and feed the girl, and also attempts to communicate with her without success. Suspecting she is the victim of some sort of abuse Benny contacts social services, but his call is unsuspectingly intercepted by the laboratory which dispatches Agent Connie Frazier to investigate. Agent Frazier murders Benny, posing the scene as a suicide to throw off suspicion. Later, when Chief Jim Hopper comes to investigate, we learn that he was a friend of Benny, the grill's gentle giant.

The real-life location used for Benny's Burgers is actually a restaurant called Tiffany's Kitchen located in Atlanta, Georgia.

BIKES

Like everything else in *Stranger Things*, the boys' bikes were carefully chosen to fit its 1983 setting. Isle of Man-based prop master Lynda Reiss was tasked with picking out the props for the series. Armed with a reported budget of $220,000 she sourced most of her items from flea markets, yard sales and eBay. The bikes were particularly difficult to source, especially as she was required to find sixteen in all. That's right – for each of the bikes seen on-screen, Reiss also had to find a backup bike, a stunt bike and a backup stunt bike: sixteen bikes in total.

Finding sixteen period-appropriate bikes is easier said than done, so the prop team ended up with a mixture of original models and custom-built rides, made up of a mishmash of banana seat bikes and retro BMXs that will be familiar to anyone who got around using pedal power in the early 1980s.

'Mike's bike is actually a reproduction,' Reiss told wired.com in July 2016. 'We aged them all up and taped them. With Dustin's bike, we decided he was sort of a klutz. So we painted his bike but never finished it, and that's why his bike is two colors.'

But the bikes aren't just there to engage viewers' nostalgia; they were also, like many of the background elements of *Stranger Things*, there to evoke iconic 1980s movies. Think bikes on the big screen and you'll no doubt be drawn to the likes of Spielberg's 1982 magnum opus *E.T.* or *The Goonies*, which Spielberg produced. In both of these films bikes play an important role. Indeed the bike in *E.T.* became so iconic that Spielberg chose it for the logo of his production company Amblin Entertainment.

It's perhaps no surprise, then, to see the Duffer Brothers directly reference *E.T.*'s use of bikes in *Stranger Things*' seventh episode, as the boys attempt to escape the authorities. The sequence, which sees the boys attempt to outrun the nefarious employees of Hawkins Energy, involves a section where a bicycle-bound El uses her telekinetic powers to flip an oncoming van. It evokes the moment in *E.T.* when the visiting alien uses his powers to make Elliott and his friends' bikes go airborne, consequently evading capture from the police.

'We originally did not have a bike chase planned for this season,' the Duffer Brothers told *Entertainment Weekly* in July 2016. 'It's obviously very reminiscent of *E.T.*, and we tried to resist the impulse, we honestly did. But we're only human.'

Of course, there's also plenty of symbolism tied up in the humble bicycles the boys use to ferry themselves around the town of Hawkins. Chief Hopper sums it up best when he says, 'A bike is like a Cadillac to these kids,' on discovering Will Byers' abandoned BMX.

Hopper's comparison with a car is no accident. On both the small and silver screen bikes are the ultimate symbol of freedom, especially for kids getting their first taste of the excitement and dangers that come with them. Whether it's *The Goonies*, *E.T.*, *BMX Bandits*, or more recent fare like JJ Abrams' *Super 8*, the bike has symbolised adventure. And, given *Stranger Things*' fascination with themes such as growing up, the youngsters' choice of pedal-powered propulsion is no accident.

'THE BODY'

'The Body' is the name of the fourth episode from the first season of *Stranger Things*. Its title refers to the discovery of the fake body of Will Byers at the Hawkins quarry, but it's also a nod to the Stephen King short story of the same name. The episode was directed by Shawn Levy and written by Justin Doble and represents something of a turning point for many of the characters.

The episode itself revolves around the funeral for Will; his elder brother Jonathan prepares for the service while Joyce continues to refuse to accept the apparent death of her son. However just as you begin to doubt Joyce's claims, it is shown that she is in fact telling the truth. Not only does Joyce make contact with Will through the wall of her home, but the boys and Eleven also listen in on her conversation with her missing son through the ham radio. Meanwhile Hopper breaks into the morgue to discover that Will's body is a fake, and Nancy and Jonathan piece together a photograph that seems to show the same monster that Joyce has described to her son.

BODY DOUBLE (1984)

Body Double is a 1984 film directed by legendary filmmaker Brian de Palma. An erotic thriller which was heavily influenced by Alfred Hitchcock movies such as *Rear Window*, the movie follows an out-of-work actor who spies through a telescope on a beautiful woman in a neighbouring apartment.

So what does this have to do with *Stranger Things*? While Jonathan's photography undoubtedly draws its inspirations from a host of movie peepers, the moment when he peers through the blinds via his zoom lens at

Nancy losing her virginity is a direct reference to *Body Double*, almost perfectly mimicking the film's original poster.

BOOMBOX

Another example of retro technology snuck into *Stranger Things* is the Panasonic RX-5090. An iconic piece of 1980s memorabilia, the boombox can be spotted in the show's second episode when The Clash's 'Should I Stay or Should I Go?' starts mysteriously playing in Will Byers's room.

BRENNER, DR MARTIN

The Big Bad of the *Stranger Things* universe – if we overlook the terrifying flesh eating monster – is Dr Martin Brenner, the silver-haired scientist and the centre of the mysterious goings on at Hawkins National Laboratory. Otherwise known as the 'Bad Man', Brenner is played in the series by acting veteran Matthew Modine, who previously appeared in films like Stanley Kubrick's *Full Metal Jacket* and TV shows including *Weeds*. Regularly seen on screen sporting his charcoal suit, black tie and black trenchcoat, Brenner is the Senior Research Scientist and Director of the research centre – which, in layman's terms, means he's the boss.

Relatively little is known about the character's history but we do glean, over the series, that he was involved in the Project MKUltra, a controversial CIA-backed experiment which attempted to develop mind-control techniques. As part of Brenner's experiments during the programme, test subjects were given psychedelic drugs, as well as punished with sleep deprivation, malnourishment and physical and mental abuse. One of Dr Brenner's subjects was Terry Ives, who gave birth to a daughter, Jane, during the course of the experiments.

When Project MKUltra was shut down, Dr Brenner took Terry's daughter from her to continue his experiments, covering up her existence so well that a lawsuit filed by Terry was dismissed due to lack of evidence. Dr Brenner played a crucial role in her upbringing as we see during flashbacks, which show her referring to her grey-haired captor as 'Papa'.

Despite his role as her father figure, Dr Brenner continues to experiment on Eleven in order to explore the limits of her telekinetic and telepathic activities. We are shown snippets of their time together, with Dr Brenner attempting to hone her abilities, often using cruelty as a way of perfecting her concentration. We also see that it is Dr Brenner who is responsible for opening the gate to the Upside Down. During one operation, when he uses a sensory deprivation tank in order for Eleven to spy on a Russian agent, she encounters the Monster. Even though the girl is clearly terrified, Brenner coerces her back into the tank in order to make contact with the Monster again, causing the gate to open.

The dimensional rift is just the beginning of Dr

Brenner's evil deeds, however. After Eleven's escape he shows that he will stop at nothing to recapture his prized guinea pig – even going so far as to falsify Will Byers' death. We can also assume that it is on his orders that Agent Connie Frazier kills Benny Hammond in order to cover up Eleven's escape. His disregard for human life is also shown as he sends one of the Hawkins Laboratory team through the gate in order to explore what is on the other side.

Later in the series Dr Brenner enters the field himself, leading the team who chase down Eleven and the boys on the streets of Hawkins, and later at the Middle School after Hopper tips him off to their location. During his attempt to recapture Eleven, Dr Brenner is attacked by the Monster in a moment of grizzly schadenfreude, though at the end of the series it is unclear whether he was killed in the attack or if he was somehow able to escape.

BROWN, MILLIE BOBBY

Millie Bobby Brown, who plays Eleven, was born to British parents in Malaga, Spain on 19 February 2004. One of three siblings – she has an older sister Paige (23), an older brother Charlie (18), and a younger sister Ava (4) – Millie was just four years old when her parents moved the family to Bournemouth in Dorset, England. There she attended Pokesdown Community Primary School where she regularly appeared in school plays, even going so far as to describe herself as a 'drama queen'.

In 2012 her family upped sticks again, this time emigrating to Orlando, Florida to set up a tooth whitening business. It was there that Millie really began to nurture her talent. She enrolled in stage school, spending hours every Saturday dancing, singing and acting. A talent-spotting agent suggested to her family that they relocate to Hollywood to be closer to the action. So they did.

In 2013, just three months after moving to Los Angeles with her family, Millie landed her first role on ABC's Lewis Carroll-inspired *Once Upon A Time in Wonderland*. A spin-off of the network's long running fantasy drama *Once Upon A Time*, Millie was cast as young Alice, but appeared in just two episodes before the show was axed in 2014.

Next she landed a leading role in *Intruders*, a BBC America production that turned out to be another one-season wonder. Based on the novel of the same name by British author Michael Marshall Smith, the series followed an LA detective who investigates a secret society which pursues immortality by forcibly implanting their souls into other peoples' bodies after their deaths. Millie was cast as Madison, a nine-year-old girl who serves as the vessel to enable an infamous serial killer to come back to life.

Intruders saw Millie work with some top notch talent including English actors John Simm and James Frain. There was also plenty of talent behind the camera, involving the likes of *The X Files'* Glen Morgan and *The Blair Witch Project's* Eduardo Sánchez. However, despite its talented cast and intriguing premise, the reviews of the series weren't kind – many criticised its plotlines for being confusing, and with dwindling ratings it was no surprise when the show was cancelled after one season. The silver lining for Millie, though, was that she was one of *Intruders*' highlights, and received rave reviews – entertainment industry bible *Variety* described her as 'phenomenal'.

After *Intruders* Millie found bit part roles in US TV staples such as *NCIS*, *Modern Family* and *Grey's Anatomy*, but no leading roles. It wasn't for the want of trying however and the actress came close on numerous occasions, most notably being shortlisted for Steven Spielberg's *BFG* adaptation before missing out at the last hurdle.

Things had not gone according to plan for Millie and her family during this period. 'It was very hard,' she told the *Mail on Sunday*. 'There were lots of tears along the way.' Millie's parents had sold everything to move out West and the family was in dire financial straits. Things got so bad that her sister Paige moved back home and, just to survive, her parents had to borrow money from her manager Melanie Greene.

By the summer of 2015, and with her parents close to bankruptcy, Millie had moved back to England. While her family stayed with an aunt to try and get back on their feet, Millie continued to audition for roles but also continued to struggle, reaching her lowest point after some particularly cutting remarks from one casting agent. 'She said I was too mature and grown up,' Millie told the *Mail on Sunday*. 'She made me cry.' However things were soon about to turn around for the young star – just later that same day she auditioned for *Stranger Things*. After impressing the production crew it wasn't long before she was back on a plane to the US to begin filming her role as Eleven.

Millie prepared for her role by watching iconic 1980s films. Before filming began, the Duffer Brothers asked her to watch *Stand By Me*, *The Goonies*, *Poltergeist* and *E.T.* They hadn't, however, told her anything about her role and it was only after her family got to Atlanta that they found out she'd have to shave her head.

Millie took the head-shaving news in her stride, showing a staggeringly mature attitude for such a young actress. 'I was like, "Mum, let's just cut it off, it grows back, it's not permanent and I need to show how much I'm involved with this character and how much I'm involved with the show,"' Millie told the magazine *SciFiNow*. 'I wanted the best for the show and if that's what I had to do, then that's what I had to do!'

When it came to actually cutting her hair, the Duffer Brothers asked Millie to channel the attitude of another famous actress who had lopped off her locks for a screen role. 'I sat in the chair, and, one by one, they cut it off,' Millie told *IndieWire*. 'I was like, "Oh no. What have I done?" And they told me, "I want you to have the mind-frame of Charlize Theron in *Mad Max*." And we did this sort of split-screen of her and me, and the resemblance was amazing! I thought, "Wow, that's such an amazing way to put it, you know?" It was the best decision I've ever, ever made.' In August 2016 Millie tweeted a video of her getting her head shaved. It received more than 100,000 likes and 44,000 retweets.

But Millie brought much more than a shaved head to her role as Eleven. Her powerful portrayal of the character led the *New Yorker* to describe it as 'a career-launching performance'. Pop culture website Vulture was even more effusive in its praise: 'As the enigmatic, often silent Eleven, a girl with telekinetic powers and the closely shaven haircut of a cancer patient undergoing chemo, Brown conveys a range of emotions – fear, confusion, raw fury – using only her eyes and a face that itself seems like a portal into some parallel universe. In such a Spielbergian project, the Duffer brothers undoubtedly wanted their Eleven to have a genuine Spielberg face. Brown's definitely got one; you watch her and you're reminded of Henry Thomas in *E.T.* and Samantha Morton in *Minority Report* all at once.'

Following this critical acclaim Millie was also recognized on the awards circuit, landing a nomination for Favorite Sci-Fi/Fantasy TV Actress at 2017's People's Choice awards as well as nods for Outstanding Performance by a Female Actor in a Drama Series and Outstanding Performance by an Ensemble in a Drama Series at the 2017 Screen Actors Guild Awards.

Given her standout performance on *Stranger Things*

it's perhaps no surprise that Millie has been bombarded with job offers since the series aired. In January 2017 it was confirmed that the actress had landed her first movie role when it was announced that she'd star in *Godzilla: King of the Monsters*, a sequel to the 2014 monster movie *Godzilla*.

Millie's career has also started to blossom in other areas. In 2016 she appeared in the music video for 'Find Me' by English EDM outfit Sigma. In January 2017 she was also unveiled as the new face of Calvin Klein's By Appointment brand, so becoming, at the age of twelve, the youngest ever model to front a campaign for the iconic fashion brand. Announcing her involvement on Instagram, she wrote: 'I am so honored to be a part of this – "A cast of distinct individuals brings the idea to life: Strength of character is key. Whether famous or unknown, all are treated equally" – Calvin Klein By Appointment.'

Despite her success in front of of the cameras, away from them Millie seems like any other teenage girl. She apparently loves roast dinners and, like her dad and brother, is a passionate supporter of Liverpool Football Club. She's also into boxing, telling Vulture: 'I do Thai boxing Mondays, jujitsu Tuesdays and Thursdays, and Wednesdays I do boxing with Mark – he was a world champion at one point. I absolutely love it. I actually have a punching bag outside in my garden. I'm obsessed with working out. I eat like a pig so it kind of makes up for that.' Also a talented singer, Millie is a huge music fan whose favourite artists include Adele, Ed Sheeran and Amy Winehouse.

The actress has become firm friends with her *Stranger Things* co-star Winona Ryder, with whom she was spotted in the front row of the Coach show at New York Fashion Week. Speaking to *SciFiNow* Millie said: 'Winona's just a phenomenal, amazing actress! We have a really good friendship, and because she was a child actress and she cut her hair, and I'm a child actress and I cut my hair, I think we just have so much in common.'

Winona isn't her only famous friend, however. Millie describes her co-stars Gaten Matarazzo, Caleb McLaughlin, Noah Schnapp and Finn Wolfhard as her 'big brothers'. She is also close friends with Maddie Ziegler who became famous after starring in Lifetime's reality behemoth *Dance Moms*.

In May 2017 Millie Bobby Brown made history by becoming the the inaugural winner of the new gender-neutral acting category at the MTV Movie and TV Awards in LA. After beating the likes of Emilia Clarke (*Game of Thrones*), Jeffrey Dean Morgan (*The Walking Dead*) and Donald Glover (*Atlanta*) in the highly-competitive category, she took to the stage to receive her prize, and even shed a tear as she delivered an emotional acceptance speech.

'I want to thank the cast and crew [of *Stranger Things*] for being my second family – you guys, I love you,' she said as the audience cheered her on. 'And I want to thank my family... and my mum and dad for being so supportive.'

Finally, she praised the Duffer Brothers for creating the character that has shot her to stardom:

'They've created a bad-ass, female, iconic character that I've got the honour to play.'

BULLIES

Bullying is a theme that runs throughout *Stranger Things* but Hawkins' most memorable teenage tormentors are Troy (Peyton Wich) and James (Cade Jones) who continually confront Mike and co. throughout the first season. The duo represent the atypical American bully, characters who regular feature in 1980s-era coming-of-age dramas from John Hughes' high school classics like *Weird Science* and *Pretty in Pink* to small screen fare such as *The Wonder Years* and the 1999 series *Freaks and Geeks*.

In many ways Troy and James resemble an almost cartoonish caricature of school-age tormentors that have been committed to screen. They patrol the playground never missing an opportunity to mock our heroes for everything from their appearance to the death of a best friend. Troy shows that he is the one willing to go to more extreme lengths to assault his victims, holding Dustin at knifepoint and threatening to cut out his teeth during episode six of the show's first season. Indeed, had it not been for Eleven's intervention, Troy would also have forced Mike to jump to his inevitable death in order to protect his friend.

Despite the extremity of their actions, for the boys the bullies have become a part of their day-to-day life, a symptom of existing on the nerdier end of the social spectrum during the 1980s. They even have a name for them, 'mouth breathers', which perfectly encapsulates their understanding of their oppressors' motivations. For the audience, though, Troy and James serve as another reason to root for our heroes. Everyone can relate to the boys' suffering and Troy and James become more relatable adversaries than the 'bad men' or the faceless creature from the Upside Down.

Hawkins Middle School's resident mouth breathers also play a part in delivering some of the series' more fist pump-worthy moments as the Duffer Brothers deliver the kind of revenge fantasy anyone who has been bullied can relate to. Of course, getting one over your adolescent oppressors is a common theme in popular culture, but few bullies have been vanquished in quite such unusual ways as Troy and James in *Stranger Things*.

Their first moment of comeuppance takes place during the assembly organised in the wake of Will Byers' apparent death. After a fight breaks out between Troy and Mike, Eleven steps in, using her powers to make Troy wet himself in front of the entire school. As if that excruciatingly embarrassing moment wasn't enough, she later uses her telekinetic abilities to break the bully's arm after he threatens her friends.

But Troy and James aren't the only bullies in *Stranger Things*. The show is filled with them, whether it's Dr Brenner, Lonnie Byers, or even Steve and Tommy who smash Jonathan Byers' camera in an act of adolescent aggression.

BUONO, CARA

Cara Buono is an American actress who plays the role of Karen Wheeler, matriarch of the Wheeler household in *Stranger Things*. Born in New York in 1974, Buono was a regular on the stage before her transition to the silver screen. Her debut role came opposite Ethan Hawke and Jeremy Irons in the 1992 drama *Waterland*.

Buono's career has tended to focus on indie films with roles in offbeat productions including *Next Stop Wonderland* (1998), *Two Ninas* (1999) and *Chutney Popcorn* (1999), although mainstream recognition came via Ang Lee's *Hulk* (2003). As well as starring in front of it, Buono has also worked extensively behind the camera writing, directing and producing films.

Stranger Things isn't Buono's first time appearing in a critically acclaimed TV series either. The actress starred as the wife of a mobster in the HBO smash hit *The Sopranos*, while her role as Dr Faye Miller in the fourth series of *Mad Men* earned her an Emmy Nomination for Outstanding Guest Actress in a Drama Series in 2011.

BYERS, JOYCE

Played by Hollywood heavyweight Winona Ryder, Joyce Byers is one of the major characters from the first season of *Stranger Things*. As the mother of the missing Will Byers her emotional turmoil and pain is front and centre throughout, but it is her refusal to give up on her son, and her relentless quest for answers that provides the narrative with its driving force.

Joyce is a single mother who works long hours – often during holiday times – to support her family. She works at Melvin's General Store in downtown Hawkins, and is well known to local residents. She was formerly married to Lonnie, and it is insinuated that she also has a romantic history with Jim Hopper, whom she teams up with to save Will from the Upside Down during the season finale.

It is Joyce who raises the alarm over Will's disappearance and who first makes contact with her missing son. She hears him through the phone, only for it to short circuit a few moments after. Later she works out that Will is trying to contact her by using electricity and eventually sees something trying to burst through from the Upside Down in the wall of her home. We learn that she has a history of anxiety and so it is perhaps no surprise that people around her question her actions as she takes an axe to her house, daubs paint on its walls, and strings fairy lights up in every room.

However her commitment to finding her lost son is never questioned. Even when faced with the body that was found in the town's quarry Joyce's faith never waivers, despite all evidence to the contrary, and her commitment forces Hopper to investigate and eventually uncover the conspiracy conducted by Dr Brenner and the Hawkins Laboratory team. Finally, during the series finale, she teams up with a ragtag group made up of Jonathan, Nancy, Hopper, Eleven and Will's friends to find and rescue Will, going so far as entering the Upside Down in order to find and bring back her son.

She is a classic Mama Bear who is fiercely protective of her family, but despite her maternal instincts she is far from flawless. Joyce chain-smokes cigarettes and it's hinted that her combative relationship with her estranged husband somewhat scarred Jonathan and Will during their younger years. During Will's disappearance she also withdraws from the world around her, leading to seventeen-year-old Jonathan having to step into the breach and organise his younger brother's funeral. Indeed both Lonnie and Hopper directly question her maternal abilities at some point, perhaps prompting viewers to do the same.

Like so many aspects of the show Joyce's origins owe a lot to the 1980s entertainment that inspired the Duffer Brothers to write *Stranger Things* in the first place. Writing for The AV Club, journalist Molly Eichel remarked that 'Joyce comes from a grand tradition of fierce sci-fi/horror mothers who go to incredible lengths to save or protect their children. These women, who exist in predominantly male-geared genres, are fierce, yet feminine, committing inhuman acts in the service of their offspring.'

Her existence owes a lot to matriarchs who were commonplace in 1980s movies, with the likes of *E.T.*, *Close Encounters of the Third Kind,* and *The Goonies* being the most obvious touch points for single mothers who stand up for their children no matter what. In science fiction terms there are also parallels with iconic female protagonists such as the *Terminator* franchise's Sarah Connor or *Alien*'s Ellen Ripley.

Many critics, however, have noted the similarities with the 1982 classic *Poltergeist.* The Duffer Brothers have repeatedly admitted that the Steven Spielberg-scripted horror was a big influence on *Stranger Things* and the two projects share a number of similarities. Both focus on small children with other worldly powers who are trapped in an alternate dimension – but the most striking similarity lies between Joyce Byers and *Poltergeist*'s Diane Freeling. Both mothers refuse to give up on their offspring and are convinced of their existence even when they are trapped in other dimensions. Both women also find a means of breaking that dimensional divide: Joyce communicating through electricity while Diane communicates with her missing daughter through the television.

BYERS, JONATHAN

Older brother to Will and dutiful son to Joyce, Jonathan is the de-facto 'Man of the House' in the Byers household.

On the night of Will's disappearance Jonathan has been working late attempting to earn extra money to support his mother, something that he continues to do as she struggles to cope with her youngest son's disappearance.

Even though he is only seventeen years old, Jonathan, played by Charlie Heaton, is wise beyond his years. He assists the police in the search for his missing brother, produces posters to plaster around Hawkins and even takes to the woods himself in an attempt to find some clue as to Will's whereabouts. After discovering the truth about Will's disappearance Jonathan continues with his all-action approach in an attempt to kill the Monster that abducted him, working with Nancy to set a trap in the Byers household that eventually maims the bloodthirsty beast.

Like his younger brother, Jonathan is something of an outsider, the consummate loner who spends his time looking at others from out of the darkness. We learn that, from the age of six, he has dreamt about escaping from Hawkins and of going to New York University. Like Will he is also sensitive, a point that is proved emphatically after we learn that he sobbed for nine days after his father forced him to shoot a rabbit as a child. He is also artistic, with a passion for music and a flair for photography. Regularly armed with his trusty Pentax MX SLR camera, his inquisitive nature got the better of him when he used a telephoto lens and turned into a Peeping Tom as he shot photos of Nancy at Steve's house. His salvation, though, comes when those same photos eventually convince the crew of the creature's existence and help them to formulate a plan to defeat it.

He is the consummate big brother, the type of guy who is just as likely to pick you up from your friend's house after a festive game of Dungeons & Dragons as he is to attempt to beat seven shades of Eggo out of a faceless creature from another dimension with a nail-spiked baseball bat. He also gets big brother points for introducing Will to classic punk and offering words of wisdom like 'You shouldn't like things because people tell you you're supposed to.'

By the end of the first season it seems as if Jonathan has developed friendships with Nancy and Steve, though they will no doubt be strained in future episodes, considering he is in love with the former and he beat the hell out of the latter for taunting his missing brother.

BYERS, LONNIE

Played by Ross Partridge, Lonnie Byers is a recurring character in the first season of *Stranger Things*. Born and raised in Hawkins, Lonnie is Joyce's estranged husband and father of both Jonathan and Will.

It is implied that Lonnie was an alcoholic and a drug addict who was at best negligent, and at worst abusive to his family. We are told that he forced Jonathan to shoot and kill a rabbit when his son was just ten years old and that he would regularly call Will a 'fag'. After his divorce from Joyce, Lonnie moved to Indianapolis where he lives with his girlfriend Cynthia and shows little interest in maintaining contact with his sons until he hears about Will's disappearance.

In the opening episode of the series, Joyce attempts to call Lonnie as she frantically searches for information on Will's disappearance. In episode two, 'The Weirdo on Maple Street', Jonathan skips school and drives to Indianapolis to make sure Will isn't with his father. In this episode we get a brief window into Lonnie's world. From his unkempt appearance to the rundown shack he shares with Cynthia, and even the way he aggressively greets Jonathan, whom he first thinks is an intruder, his life is a world away from the suburban bliss of Hawkins.

We also get a glimpse of Lonnie's attitude to his offspring as he acts indifferently towards Jonathan and seems more interested in how Joyce has described him to their sons than in Will's disappearance. The episode also introduces us to Lonnie's prized possession, a 1972 Oldsmobile 442, an immaculately maintained muscle car that highlights the deadbeat dad's skewed priorities. The Oldsmobile is also an important plot point as, later in the season, Jonathan breaks into his father's car in order to steal his handgun as he embarks on an attempt to kill the Monster from the Upside Down.

Lonnie returns to Hawkins later in the season following the discovery of Will's body at the town quarry. He attends Will's funeral and plans to sleep on Joyce's couch for a few days in an apparent attempt to support his ex-wife. After seeing the state of the Byers home, where Joyce has strung up endless Christmas lights and daubed paint on the walls, Lonnie tries to convince his former partner to seek psychiatric help and even tells Jonathan that his mother is sick.

At first it appears that Lonnie is making up for lost time, that his mourning for Will's death is leading to him attempting to reconcile with what is left of his family, in an effort to make good. However his true intentions are eventually revealed when Joyce discovers a flyer for a lawyer who specialises in accidental death and injury lawsuits. After she confronts her former husband, we learn that Lonnie plans to sue the quarry in an attempt to profit from his son's death. Enraged by his actions Joyce tells her ex-husband to leave, and during the ensuing argument he calls her a mess and blames her for Will's disappearance before driving away. At the end of the season it is not known where he has gone or what has happened to him.

If Lonnie's screen time in the series felt a little stilted, that is probably because it was. The character was meant to play a much larger role in the first season's finale but his action had to be cut short due to the narrative constraints of the show. Speaking to Alan Sepinwall in Uproxx in July 2016, Matt Duffer said: 'Lonnie, who is Joyce's douchey ex-husband, was going to play a bigger part in the climax, but we ended up giving that part to Steve Harrington [the character of Nancy Wheeler's boyfriend]. But that was narrative reasons dictating that, not story reasons.'

BYERS, WILL

The boy whose disappearance started it all, Will Byers (played by Noah Schnapp) is the twelve-year-old son of Joyce and Lonnie Byers and the younger brother of Jonathan. Like his brother, Will is shown to be a sensitive child with a strong relationship with his family.

He is friends with Lucas, Dustin and Mike. Like the other boys he is a keen member of the school's A.V. Club and is a regular competitor in the annual science fair (which we are told the boys always win). Will is also interested in music, thanks to his brother Jonathan, who introduced him to artists like The Clash, Joy Division, The Smiths and David Bowie through mixtapes that he would give to him.

Will's interest in popular culture, though, extends beyond music. He has a poster of Steven Spielberg's *Jaws* hanging in his room and bets on a bike race with his friend Dustin for a copy of a Marvel's X-Men comic. Like the other boys, Will is also a gamer who is desperate to get his hands on an Atari console for Christmas. Away from video games he enjoys regular Dungeons & Dragons sessions with his friends; his character is a wizard who goes by the magical moniker of 'Will the Wise'.

Although Will is abducted and taken to the Upside Down in the show's opening episode, we get to learn a lot about him via his friends and family, as well as flashbacks to his previous life in Hawkins. We learn that Will is a talented artist who can draw in exceptional detail despite his young age, something that Joyce recalls when Hopper shows her a child's drawing he found in the laboratory. Will's creativity can also been seen in Castle Byers, the fort he built out in the woods which serves as his shelter during his time in the Upside Down.

For a twelve year old boy, Will is also incredibly resourceful, more than living up to his 'Wise' alter-ego from the world of Dungeons & Dragons. His ability to escape from the Monster in the Upside Down for more than a week is testament to this, especially compared with the fate of both Barb and of Shepard, the Hawkins Lab employee who died almost instantly after entering through the gate. He is good at hiding, as his brother Jonathan tells us, but his survival instincts go well beyond that, and it is only when he has grown weak from hunger and the toxicity of the alternate dimension that he is eventually captured. Will's ingenuity is also demonstrated in his repeated attempts to contact his mother, at first using the telephone and later electricity in order to convince her that he is still alive.

While Will's whereabouts are obviously the principal mystery of the series, it is the character's sexuality that became one of the most discussed topics among its fanbase on Internet messageboards and forums. People picked up on several references scattered throughout the series such as Lonnie's jibes that his son was a 'fag' as well as school bully Troy's repeated homophobic slurs about Will during his absence. This speculation formed the basis for an essay scribbled in *Advocate*, a bi-monthly magazine on LGBTQ issues. Written by Daniel Reynolds the essay explores whether homophobia is the real monster in the *Stranger Things* series. 'There's also the matter of what the characters call the "Upside Down", an alternate dimension where the monster lives,' Reynolds writes. 'Characters who are outsiders – Will as well as Barb, the "unsung and forgotten hero" of *Stranger Things*, as Vulture dubbed her – are dragged there and left to die. It's a dark, cold, and lifeless version of the real world, and a potent metaphor for the closet.'

Noah Schnapp, the twelve-year-old actor who plays Will Byers, actually engaged with fans via social media on the subject of his character's sexuality. Posting on Instagram in October 2016 he wrote: 'So I thought it would be time to jump into the conversation. I've been reading stuff for a while. I think everyone here is missing the point. An author called Gary Schmidt came to speak at our school this week and he said that good stories aren't supposed to leave you with answers because then you never question yourself and you forget about it. A good book, or a good show, leaves a lot of unanswered questions but makes you think. Which is what you are all doing. For me, Will being gay or not is besides the point. *Stranger Things* is a show about a bunch of kids who are outsiders and find each other because they have been bullied in some way or are different. Does being sensitive, or a loner, or a teenager who likes photography, or a girl with red hair and big glasses, make you gay? I'm only 12 but I do know we all relate to being different. And that's why I think the Duffers wrote the show the way they did. So you can ask all these questions. I hope the real answer never comes out!'

At the end of the first season Will is rescued from the Upside Down by Joyce and Hopper, and after convalescing in hospital returns home in time for Christmas. Despite the apparent happy ending, though, all is not as it seems. The finale ends with Will regurgitating a slug-like creature that showed everything may not be as A-OK as it seems on the surface. It seems Season 2 will focus on how Will's week spent in an alternate dimension has affected him.

'We love the idea that [the Upside Down] is an environment that is not a great place for a human being to be living in,' they said in an interview with *Variety* in July 2016. 'Will's been there for an entire week, and it's had some kind of effect on him, both emotionally and perhaps physically. The idea is he's escaped this nightmare place, but has he really? That's a place we wanted to go and potentially explore in season two. What effect does living in there for a week have on him? And what has been done to him? It's not good, obviously.'

CALLAHAN

Played by John Paul Reynolds, Officer Callahan is part of the Hawkins Police Department. Alongside Chief Jim Hopper and Officer Powell, Callahan is part of the team that investigates Will Byers' disappearance. With his curly mop of brown hair and thick rimmed glasses, the character serves as comic relief delivering some of the series' best throwaway lines and inappropriate comments. His name could be a reference to Father Callahan, a character in Stephen King's *The Dark Tower* series.

CAROL

Played by Chelsea Talmadge, Carol is a recurring character from the first season of *Stranger Things*. The

Hawkins High School student debuts in episode two when she attends a party at Steve Harrington's house alongside her boyfriend Tommy H. She is the archetypal 1980s mean girl, a teenage terror whose screen time is divided between sideways glances, sniggers and stinging criticisms. At first she is shown as a close friend of Steve's but by the end of the season, after goading Jonathan about his brother's disappearance, she is alienated from his social circle.

CARPENTER, JOHN

Steven Spielberg is not the only director whose shadow looms large over *Stranger Things.* There is also John Carpenter whose influence on modern filmmaking, especially in horror, cannot be overestimated, thanks to such classics as *Halloween* (1978), *Escape From New York* (1981) and *The Thing* (1982).

From the eerie suburban landscapes, to teenagers beset by supernatural threats, Carpenter's influence on the Duffer Brothers can be seen throughout the first season. Discussing their inspirations in an interview with IGN in July 2016, Ross Duffer said: 'Obviously the influences are all over the show, whether it's Spielberg's stuff or John Carpenter or the novels of Stephen King. And I think for us looking at it, it's like, "What is it about these stories that resonated so much with us when we were growing up?" And I think really what it is, what connects all of them even though tonally sometimes they're different -- but what really connects them is that these very ordinary people encountering these very extraordinary things. So I think those were the initial conversations, of can we get back to that style of storytelling?'

As well as these themes, there are also some very specific references from some of his films scattered throughout the first season of the show. For instance, the boys' use of the A.V. Club's ham radio to contact Will is a nice nod to Carpenter's 1980 movie *The Fog*. There are also some more direct references to the same director's *The Thing*. Indeed Mike has a poster for the 1982 classic in his basement, and Mr Clarke is shown watching the film itself when the boys call him at 10pm on a weekend to ask his advice on how to build a sensory deprivation tank.

Carpenter's synth-heavy scores for movies such as *Halloween* and *Assault on Precinct 13* also inspired the sound of *Stranger Things*. As well as being entirely period-appropriate, the sound of the Upside Down is laden with terror, recalling some of Carpenter's best composing, as well as more modern movies such as Nicolas Winding Refn's *Drive (2011)*.

'Before we were even talking about John Carpenter, we were inspired by film composers moving back into the electronic space,' the show's co-creator Matt Duffer told *Complex* in August 2016. 'We were really into what Cliff Martinez did with *Drive*, and what Trent Reznor and Atticus Ross were doing with David Fincher. We wanted the Stephen King DNA, the John Carpenter DNA. We thought, let's get more into electronic music.'

CARRIE (1976)

The story of a young girl with a sheltered upbringing and telekinetic powers, there's more than a few similarities between *Stranger Things*'s Eleven and Stephen King's titular character from his debut novel. Indeed the Duffer Brothers have been open about their inspiration and have gone on record to express their fandom for King's 1974 novel and the subsequent 1976 movie.

For the uninitiated, *Carrie* tells the story of a sixteen-year-old girl from a small town who is repeatedly bullied at school. Her home life isn't much better – her widowed mother is a fanatical Christian fundamentalist who repeatedly abuses her daughter. After a particularly brutal bout of locker room bullying Carrie discovers she has telephonic and telekinetic powers, which she later uses to kill her schoolmates and her mother, after being embarrassed at the school prom.

Carrie was Stephen King's first published novel and helped to launch the author to stardom. The film adaptation, directed by Brian De Palma, starred Sissy Spacek in the title role, John Travolta and Piper Laurie and has gone on to become one of the most influential horror movies ever made.

Stranger Things doesn't go to quite as extreme lengths as Stephen King's story, but alongside Eleven's similarities with her telekinetic counterpart, there's also a nice reference to the film in Chapter Five when Nancy Wheeler thrusts her hand through a wall of goo as she attempts to escape from a portal to the Upside Down. It echoes the moment at the end of De Palma's movie when Sissy Spacek's hand reaches through the soil from her grave.

CARS

Like everything else in *Stranger Things*, the cars had to be carefully curated to make them as period appropriate to the 1980s as possible. One rogue Prius or a late model Japanese import and the entire spell of the series would be broken. As a result the automotive stars of the show were carefully selected to not only ensure they fit the era but also reflect the socio-economic outlook of the American midwest in 1983.

Some cars, like Joyce Byers' 1976 Ford Pinto and Jonathan's 1971 Ford LTD are entirely accurate for an all-American family who struggle to exist on the breadline. By the same token Lonnie Byers' 1972 Oldsmobile 442, the only car that is directly called out in the entire show, is entirely inappropriate for a man of his means and more of a reflection of his character than the car itself.

Other cars are also appropriate for their drivers. Take for example Steve Harrington's 1981 BMW 733i, a European import that perfectly sums up the character's rich and pampered background. With a price tag that would have been even higher than Steve's quiff, though, the car most likely belongs to his unseen father.

Some of the vehicles used in the production hark back to old favourite movies of the Duffer Brothers. Steven Spielberg's *Jaws* (1975) is no doubt a popular cultural touchpoint for the show's creators, so it's perhaps no surprise that Jim Hopper drives the same vehicle, a Chevrolet Blazer K5, as his heroic counterpart Chief Martin Brody. In fact, the police cruisers used in *Stranger Things* reference the seminal shark attack film even more directly: they were actually the exact same ones that Spielberg himself used on set.

CASTLE BYERS

Castle Byers, which doubles as the name of the opening track on the *Stranger Things* soundtrack album, is a fort built of sticks that is located in the woods near the Byers' house in Hawkins. Although the series doesn't tell us who built the makeshift structure, we do learn that it was Will's space and that he regularly retreated to the woods to read comics and draw.

Though rustic the fort does not completely lack charm. The stick structure is adorned with an American flag and three signs which read 'Castle Byers', 'All Friends Welcome', and 'Home of Will The Wise'. Inside there are creature comforts including blankets, pillows, lamps and some of Will's drawings stuck to the walls.

After Will's disappearance at the start of the series Castle Byers is the first place that Joyce looks for her son. The fort also features in a flashback in which Joyce remembers surprising Will with tickets to see *Poltergeist* at the cinema. Later, when Eleven enters the Upside Down in search of Will, we find that he has been hiding from the Demogorgon at Castle Byers, but by the time our heroine catches up with him he is very weak, and unable to run when the Monster bursts through the walls to capture him. Later, when Joyce and Hopper enter the alternate dimension in search of him they find what remains of the fort scattered in the forest.

For Will and his friends, Castle Byers is another example of their love affair with all things geek. When explaining the fort's location to Chief Hopper they tell him it is located in the 'Mirkwood', a reference to the same forest found in Tolkien's *The Hobbit*. We also learn through a flashback that the password to enter is 'Radagast', a reference to Radagast the Brown, a wizard and ally of Gandalf in the same book.

CHESTER

Though Will Byers' dog isn't actually called by his name during the first season of *Stranger Things*, the script for the pilot episode reveals his name to be Chester. Chester is introduced in the opening episode, greeting Will who is returning home after running away from the Monster. Chester is clearly delighted to see his owner, but his demeanour changes when he spots the silhouette of the Demogorgon at the door.

It's not the last time that Chester senses danger from the Upside Down. Later, when Hopper is investigating the Byers home he notices that the dog is barking continually at the shed, the place where the audience last saw Will before he was dragged to the Upside Down. Joyce, however, dismisses the behaviour as 'hunger' after Hopper asks if it's normal. Chester also sits with Joyce while she communicates with Will via the Christmas lights strewn up around her house. Although it is not explicitly mentioned in the action, there is a clear insinuation that the dog can sense something that the town's cast of human characters cannot see.

Though you'd think that the adorable mutt would have been a joy to work with, David Harbour, who plays Chief Hopper on the show, has actually admitted that it almost caused him to meltdown during filming.

'The dog was the worst on the set,' Harbour told radio shock jock Howard Stern during an interview on *The Howard Stern Wrap Up Show*. 'There was a day with this dog that was the worst actor I've ever worked with in my life. [...] The dog was just being a jerk. I never – I walked off set. I've never done that before. There's footage of me like throwing a fit, going like, "I'm gonna be in my trailer!" and just storming off. Cause the damn dog wouldn't do what it was supposed to do. It was just supposed to bark at a thing... And there was a trainer who was off camera yelling like, "C'mon, we gotta make our money, this is how we make our money!" And I was like, "This is weird."'

CIA

We learn that Dr Brenner and the Hawkins Laboratory crew were involved in CIA-sanctioned experiments in order to find people with special abilities. Though there is no proof that the CIA is directly involved in Dr Brenner's continuing work with the money and resources he and the Hawkins Laboratory have at their disposal, it's probably safe to assume that clandestine forces are counting to bankroll his research.

What's perhaps most interesting about the CIA references contained within *Stranger Things* is that they spring from real life, an example of how sometimes truth is every bit as strange as the fiction it inspires. After diligently searching through newspaper clippings Hopper uncovers Dr Brenner's involvement in Project MKUltra, a series of Cold War experiments that actually did occur.

Speaking to Vulture about the show's origins Matt Duffer confirmed that the experiments were part of their inspiration. 'When we were first starting to talk about the idea [for the show], we had talked about a paranormal-missing child story line,' he said. 'Then we were talking about some of the mysterious government experiments that we felt were happening at the tail end of the Cold War, right when rumored [projects] like MKUltra were ramping down.'

Though it sounds like the stuff conspiracy theorists' dreams are made of, the CIA's involvement with Project MKUltra is actually science fact, not science fiction. Taking place at the height of the Cold War from the 1950s to the mid 1970s, the clandestine CIA project researched everything from mind control and telepathy, to telekinesis, psychic warfare and even the type of remote viewing we see in the flashback where Eleven spies on a Russian agent.

Most of the evidence of Project MKUltra was destroyed after it was shut down in 1973, but witness testimonies, remaining records and a Senate investigation from 1977 have revealed some details about what the CIA was researching. Most notable among the findings has been the organisation's preoccupation with drugs, particularly LSD, which they thought could become the ultimate truth serum. Indeed the findings showed that many Americans were drugged without their knowledge at more than eighty institutions across the country. This is something that's echoed in the experiences of Eleven's mother Terry Ives.

Stranger Things isn't the first piece of pop culture to explore the CIA's secret MKUltra research. The experiments also influenced sci-fi shows such as *The X Files* and *Fringe* as well as playing an important role in movies such as *The Manchurian Candidate*, *The Jason Bourne* franchise and George Clooney's comedy *The Men Who Stare at Goats*.

CLARKE, SCOTT

The moustachioed science teacher from Hawkins Middle School is one of the cult favourite characters from the first season of *Stranger Things*. Played by Randall P. Havens, Scott Clarke is something of a mentor to Will's friends and plays an important part in their lives. From his role as head of the Hawkins A.V. Club to the role he plays in consoling the crew after Will's apparent demise, he's one of the most lovable adults on the show.

He also inadvertently plays an important role in the series' events. From explaining alternate dimensions to advising on the best way in which to build a sensory deprivation tank, Mr Clarke's advice helps the team to rescue their friend from the Upside Down. His straight-talking scientific explanations are also a useful source of exposition for the audience as he helps to lay out the complex scientifically theories behind things like alternate dimensions in ways the average sofa-dweller can understand.

It is Mr Clarke who comes up with the Flea and the Acrobat theory at Will's wake, which he uses to explain alternate dimensions to the boys. He is also the person who tells them how a gate might form between dimensions, tipping them onto the electromagnetic interference that led them to Hawkins Laboratory. He even explains the basics of sensory deprivation, inadvertently helping them track down Will's location in the Upside Down. Without Mr Clarke the audience would be lost, and indeed so too would Will Byers.

His influence over the children in the show is clearly visible. After all he's the adult Will's friends visit when they're in search of advice, be it scientific or otherwise. He is also shown to fan the flames of their imaginations by investing in the Heathkit ham radio for the school A.V. Club. His influence is shown during Dustin's late night call to discover the basics of sensory deprivation when he says, 'You always say we should never stop being curious, to always open any curiosity door we find.'

Mr Clarke is the wise man of the show, and the polar opposite to *Stranger Things*' other scientist of note, Dr Brenner. Whereas Brenner is cold and distant, Mr Clarke is warm and welcoming. Whereas Dr Brenner forces Eleven to explore the extents of her powers by force, Mr Clarke encourages the boys guiding their enthusiasm rather than controlling it. He is not an unapproachable authority figure. Indeed, with his boyish looks and his love of science-fiction – he is shown watching *The Thing* with his partner when Dustin calls him on a Saturday night and understands what Dungeons & Dragons' Vale of Shadows is – he seems closer to the boys than the rest of the grown-up population of Hawkins, which perhaps explains why he is the only adult they feel they can go to when they have a problem.

Speaking with fans during an AMA (Ask Me Anything) on Reddit in August 2016, Randall P. Havens spoke about how he developed his character. 'I didn't study any science for the role. The important thing for me as an actor was to find the emotional truth of a character like Mr Clarke, since I knew there was no way that I was gonna become as smart as he is. So I focused on the thing that I could understand: that Mr. Clarke identified with Mike, Dustin, Lucas and Will because he was like them when he was young. Maybe he felt like an outcast or was bullied and he wanted to create a safe place where his students felt they belonged.'

CLOSE ENCOUNTERS OF THE THIRD KIND (1977)

As babies of the eighties it's perhaps no surprise that Steven Spielberg is such an enduring influence in the Duffer Brothers' work. After all, the director who gave us *Jaws*, *E.T.*, and *Raiders of the Lost Ark* has played an important role in the lives of film fans of a certain age. It seems as if Spielberg's entire catalogue is referenced in *Stranger Things*, particularly his sci-fi classic *Close Encounters of the Third Kind*.

Released in 1977, the movie stars Richard Dreyfuss as Indiana electrician Roy Neary who, along with the government and other members of the public, experiences a close encounter with aliens. Fixated by what he's experienced, Neary becomes obsessed with UFOs and the mental image of a mountain. His behaviour puts strain on his relationship, until he realises the imagery is a message to show him the location of where the aliens are set to arrive on earth. Upon reaching the landing area he finds the army already communicating with the extraterrestrial visitors who select him to visit their mothership.

The movie was a critical and commercial success on its release, landing eight Oscar nominations including nods for Best Picture and Best Director. The film also helped to repopularise the science-fiction genre and has inspired countless homages in the forty years since its original release.

Stranger Things' most notable homage to *Close Encounters* occurs when Joyce Byers obsesses over locating her missing son, just as Jillian Guiler does over her abducted son Barry in the Spielberg movie. Joyce's alienating and destructive tendencies during her obsession also evoke Roy Neary's marital struggles. In addition, there's a pleasing visual homage when Joyce uses blinking fairy lights and electrical appliances to communicate with her missing son, directly harking back to *Close Encounters'* climax when Government forces communicate with their otherworldly visitors through a series of flashing lights.

COLEMAN, RUSSELL

Played by Tony Vaughn, Russell Coleman is the Principal of Hawkins Middle School. He is the archetypal authority figure, an educator who holds little connection to the students under his charge and is something of a contrast to Mr Clarke, the other important authority figure in the children's' lives. Principal Coleman only appears in two episodes of the show's first season, most notably in Chapter Four ('The Body') when he holds a school assembly after the apparent death of Will Byers.

CREDITS

Stranger Things' opening credit sequence carefully recalls the 1980s. Running for about a minute at the beginning of every episode the sequence is, at first glance, simplistic, with the camera slowly panning out from a series of extreme close-ups of the title logo. Far from it – the credit sequence was anything but easy to put together.

In order to truly capture the retro vibe of the show, the Duffer Brothers commissioned a company called Imaginary Forces to produce the title sequence. Imaginary Forces are no strangers to opening credits having previously worked on iconic shows such as *Mad Men* and *Boardwalk Empire*, but for *Stranger Things* they opted for a more old-fashioned approach.

Wanting to replicate the period-feel that's captured throughout the series, the team used analogue techniques that would have been prevalent in the early eighties to produce Kodalith transparencies of the film's title. Kodalith is an extremely high contrast type of film stock that was regularly used to create animations that would then be backlit and filmed to produce opening credit sequences. Before the advent of today's ubiquitous digital technologies this old-school technique came complete with imperfections, jitters and lens flares helping to create a grainy, organic feel to the sequences.

While the final credit sequence for *Stranger Things* was produced digitally, the animators took inspiration from their Kodalith prototypes, embracing the imperfections that make them feel so faithful to the period. 'We really tried to tap into that haptic quality that film has, because you're seeing light pass through film,' Michelle Dougherty, Imaginary Forces' Creative Director, said in an interview with *Wired*. 'We looked at title sequences from the past. We were looking for the inconsistencies. That's what makes it feel tangible and warm.'

The development of the *Stranger Things* sequence was heavily influenced by past credit sequences. Upon meeting the animators for the first time the Duffer Brothers spoke about their love for pulpy horror books, and name-checked Richard Greenberg, the title designer behind iconic movies such as *Superman*, *Alien* and *Dirty Dancing*. You can clearly see Greenberg's influence in the finished product, which can also be compared to early 1980s *Choose Your Own Adventure* book covers and Stephen King novels. At first glance, the title sequence could have come straight out of the early eighties, and is almost indistinguishable from influential period fare like *The Dead Zone* and *Altered States*.

What we see on screen is only half of the story of

course – the score also plays an important role in setting the scene. *Stranger Things*' theme song was composed by Kyle Dixon and Michael Stein of Austin-based band S U R V I V E. The Duffer Brothers hired the duo after hearing their synthesiser-heavy instrumentals, seeking to deliberately evoke the sort of music that directors like slasher supremo John Carpenter had used. Another reference point was the German electronic music pioneers Tangerine Dream, and their soundtrack albums in the 1970s and 1980s like *Thief* and *Sorcerer*.

The end product immediately sets the tone of the show, drawing viewers into the spooky, sci-fi setting. The synthesisers also help to add the period feeling to the action in the same way as a carefully chosen costume, car or prop.

CRITICAL RECEPTION

Upon its initial release on 15 July 2016 *Stranger Things* received overwhelmingly positive reviews from critics. The show currently holds a 95 per cent fresh rating on Internet review hub RottenTomatoes.com, ranking among the best reviewed shows of 2016.

'*Stranger Things* is the most delightful, gripping, charming, nostalgic, compulsive, edge-of-seat enter-tainment I've had in ages,' James Delingpole effused in the *Spectator*, who finished his review by saying it's like 'Spielberg given a horror makeover by Guillermo del Toro and Stephen King.'

'*Stranger Things* honors its source material in the best way possible: By telling a sweet 'n' scary story in which monsters are real but so are the transformative powers of love and fealty,' wrote the *Los Angeles Times*. 'The trappings may have been pried from the frozen ice of the Reagan administration, but the themes and the characters are timeless.'

Variety, meanwhile, praised the show's cast, particularly the younger actors on whose shoulders much of the series rests. '*Stranger Things*' greatest accomplishment may be in the casting of its younger characters,' wrote Maureen Ryan. 'Millie Brown plays a key figure in the series... All you really need to know is that she is note-perfect in her role, which requires her to be both an enigmatic object of scrutiny and a regular kid who is put in an array of confusing and difficult situations. She pulls off everything that is asked of her and more with exceptional facility and subtlety. The other young members of the cast not only avoid the kind of cloying hamminess too frequently seen among child actors, they also mesh well as a group... Without the kids' winning blend of innocence, camaraderie, sarcasm, and fear, *Stranger Things* would be a lot less binge-able.'

Elsewhere Dave Wiegand in the *San Francisco Chronicle* praised the show's escapism: '*Stranger Things* reminds us of a time marked by a kind of no-strings escapism. And as it does so, we find ourselves yearning for it because the Duffers have made it so irresistibly appealing. There may be other equally great shows to watch this summer, but I guarantee you won't have more fun watching any of them than you will watching *Stranger Things*.'

Stranger Things wasn't universally adored, however. *Entertainment Weekly* was slightly more reserved in its review, giving the series a solid B grade. While largely praising the show, and even drawing comparisons with David Lynch's uber-weird *Twin Peaks*, its reviewer ultimately wondered whether the series could move beyond its homages and references to stand on its own two feet: '*Stranger Things* has promise as a peculiar and critical historical survey of geek culture. For now, it seems content to just geek out on it.'

Lenika Cruz's review in *The Atlantic* criticised the show's treatment of Eleven whom she noted, like many girls featured in 1980s children shows, becomes little more than a token female character: '...There's a higher bar for original stories – even homages – to clear when it comes to incorporating the lessons Hollywood has learned recently about depicting female characters who are as layered as their male counterparts,' she concludes. 'For all its charms, *Stranger Things* doesn't quite meet that standard.'

Ken Tucker, reviewing the show for Yahoo!, gave an even harsher appraisal: '*Things* spends too much repetitious time trying to convince us that Mike, Dustin, and Lucas are cute kids, and the show's sense of foreshadowing when it comes to revealing something that's supposed to scare the daylights out of us becomes an exercise in tedium.' He even criticised the younger cast members who have come in for near universal praise from other critics: 'The child actors are uneven, and it's difficult to tell whether that's because of their abilities or the tiresome sentimentality sketched into the portrait of their friendship.'

These negative responses, though, were far outweighed by those critics who had lined up to heap praise on the show, and it will be interesting to see if the show continues to attract as many accolades as it moves into its second season.

CYNTHIA

Played by Stefanie Butler, Cynthia is Lonnie Byers' girlfriend and only appears in one episode of *Stranger Things*' first season. Little is known about the character, although she appears younger than Lonnie's ex-wife Joyce and it seems that there is no love lost between the two women in Lonnie's life.

D

DARLENE

The character of Darlene is only mentioned in passing – we don't even learn her last name – but we do know that she was Joyce Byers' aunt and may have suffered from mental health issues. Her existence is significant in that it creates doubt in the rest of the cast of characters when Joyce's behaviour becomes more and more manic as she attempts to make contact with her son.

DEMOGORGON

Demogorgon is the moniker used by Mike and the gang to describe the nameless Monster that wreaks havoc on the town of Hawkins in *Stranger Things*. But what is a Demogorgon and where does it come from?

The Demogorgon first crops up in the show's opening episode when the boys are playing a game of Dungeons & Dragons in Mike's basement. Mike uses the Monster as one of the main antagonists on a quest he has created for his friends ambushing their party of imaginary warriors. In an attempt to defeat the Monster, Will tries to launch a fireball using his Will the Wise alter-ego, but his dice-roll fails (he rolled a seven when he needed a fourteen) and his character fell to the Demogorgon, foreshadowing his own capture by the Upside Down later in the episode.

Like everything else seen in *Stranger Things*, the Demogorgon was a very deliberate choice of foe on the part of the Duffer Brothers. The character, described as the 'Prince of Demons' in Dungeons & Dragons literature, is widely regarded as one of the most fearsome foes players would face in the game. The monster first appeared in the D&D universe in 1976, when it appeared in the third edition of the game's box set, entitled the Eldritch Wizardry.

In the game the Demogorgon is described as 18-foot-tall with a somewhat humanoid form. It has two mandrill heads that sprout from its reptilian body and limbs that end in huge tentacles. The figure that Mike uses in his quest reflects the description, although eagle-eyed nerds will note that it isn't actually period appropriate: the figure was released as part of the Fantasy Lords series which wouldn't have been available until a full year after the events of *Stranger Things*.

The Demogorgon has led to some interesting fan

theories about the relationship between Eleven and the Monster. In Dungeons & Dragons the Demogorgon is two beings fused into one. Each being is represented by one of the monster's twin heads and while both are able to control the body, they are constantly at war with each other. Fans have suggested that Eleven and the Monster represent these two warring heads, pointing to the way in which she controls the Monster's body during the attack on Hawkins Middle School during Episode Eight and her emotional revelation to Mike in Episode Six that she believes she is a monster herself.

DEPARTMENT OF ENERGY

The Department of Energy is used as a cover for the operations of Dr Brenner and the Hawkins Laboratory team in *Stranger Things*. The use of the US department as a front in the show caused plenty of chatter among fans who wondered if its real-life counterpart had ever conducted experiments. The light-hearted chatter prompted the actual United States Department of Energy to respond to claims that it was harbouring monsters and experimenting with alternate dimensions. Published in August 2016 a blog post entitled 'What "Stranger Things" Didn't Get Quite-So-Right About the Energy Department' aimed to correct some of the show's inaccuracies about the Department of Energy.

Written by Digital Content Specialist Paul Lester the blog post confirmed that the Energy Department doesn't explore parallel universes. 'There are several scenes in the show where Hawkins Laboratory researchers don full body suits and protective gear to walk through a peculiar portal, which transports them to an alternate dimension known as "The Upside Down",' he wrote. 'While the Energy Department doesn't chart parallel universes, it does help power the exploration of new worlds. We're talking outer space, not the bizarro cosmos in *Stranger Things*.' Lester also confirmed that the Department doesn't 'mess with monsters' and that 'National Laboratory scientists aren't evil – they're actually really nice (and smart!).'

After hitting the web, the Department of Energy's post went viral among *Stranger Things* fans, but their response to the show didn't end there. After reading the blog Lachlan Markay, a journalist with the *Washington Free Beacon*, filed a Freedom of Information request to reveal all of the internal communication from the Department of Energy about *Stranger Things*. Though the request was initially something of a joke it resulted in a whole dossier of internal memos and emails being released, which Markay began to post online. The redacted emails contained emails that suggested the Department of Energy's blog post hadn't been strictly true.

One email stated that: 'It's not true that "the Energy Department doesn't explore parallel universes". We support theoretical physicists/cosmologists through the Office of Science High Energy Physics programme, some of whom almost certainly are doing a fair amount of research on parallel universes.' Another debunked the idea that the Department had never been involved in human experiments: '…there is some really eyebrow-raising stuff in the history of the atomic energy commission, in which yes, the aec [Atomic Energy Commission] did do human experiments, or participated with the military (example: soldiers were in trenches near some nuclear tests). Not sure when these ended, and to this day, we provide healthcare to people in various Pacific islands affected by nuclear tests.' Along with the more serious emails the request also revealed some more humorous correspondence between staff members complaining about *Stranger Things* spoilers.

That sense of humour seemed to seep into the Department's social media team, who responded to Markay's revelations by tweeting that 'no matter what you write, it won't bring Barb back. #JusticeForBarb.'

DEVELOPMENT

After working under the stewardship of M. Night Shyamalan on the TV mystery series *Wayward Pines*, the Duffer Brothers felt ready to produce their own TV show and sat down to cook up the idea for what would eventually turn into *Stranger Things*.

The Duffer Brothers' script which they used to pitch the show was actually very close to what we see in the series' opening episode, but that wasn't their only tool when shopping their idea to the networks. The brothers also produced a twenty-page look book designed to bring their idea for a period-set thriller to life. The book used an old Stephen King paperback cover and was filled with stills and imagery from the kind of films they reference throughout *Stranger Things*.

Despite their devotion to their idea it took a while for them to get interest from suited studio bosses. Indeed the Duffers claim that between 15 and 20 networks passed on their show before they eventually found a home on Netflix. 'The first week, I think, we had 15 pitches, and it was all passes,' Matt Duffer told the *New York Times*. 'There was a moment where we're like, "Oh, I think people aren't getting it." And then the next week, offers started to come in, and luckily Netflix understood it right away.'

Though they must be kicking themselves for their shortsightedness now, many of the networks who passed on the show were concerned that a plot centred around children but aimed at adults wouldn't work. Instead they wanted to change the aesthetic of the show, setting it up as a sheriff exploring the strange goings-on of a small town, in a similar format to David Lynch's classic *Twin Peaks*.

The Duffers stood by their idea however and in early 2015 finally found allies: Dan Cohen and Shawn Levy from 21 Laps Entertainment, a production company whose past credits include movies such as *Night at the Museum*, *Date Night* and *Real Steel*. Now armed with their script and a pair of well-known producers, the Duffers pitched *Stranger Things* to Netflix, which the brothers admitted was always the platform they wanted for the series. Netflix liked it so much that they bought the rights to the series within twenty-four hours of reading the script for the pilot, green lighting the project for a 2016 release.

DEVOTED FANS

The show instantly found a fanbase upon its release in July 2016, joining the Olympics as one of the most talked-about subjects of that summer. The surprise hit went viral, with the hashtag dominating Twitter on the weekend of its release. According to Google the show was also the most searched item in the arts and entertainment category that summer. *Stranger Things* was an overnight success, so popular with fans on its opening weekend that Netflix was inundated with angry messages on social media when the company began suffering technical issues that affected people's binge-watching.

Speaking to IGN the Duffer Brothers revealed that the sudden popularity of the show had caught them off guard. 'We turned in the last visual effects shot, walked away and then reviews and then a week later, it was all on [Netflix] and everybody was watching it,' Ross Duffer said in the interview. 'I remember waking up Friday morning to all these tweets of people that had finished the show already. It's been a whirlwind for sure and I think it's bizarre, but in the best way.'

The show's devoted fanbase quickly grew. Attracting more buzz than a bee-keeping convention, on social media the show landed more than 3 million Facebook likes in a matter of weeks and more than 666,000 followers on Twitter. Word-of-mouth also helped to build the audience, and fans flooded the Internet to theorise about the show, writing their own *Stranger Things* stories or producing artwork inspired by the series. The show's thread on Reddit has become one of the popular Internet forum's most engaged pages: fans show off everything from art and homemade posters, to specially made VHS covers and even *Stranger Things*-inspired tattoos.

The cast of the show, many of whom were experiencing fame for the first time, were taken aback by the fans. 'I knew when this was a big thing when I opened my eyes and looked out the door of my house, and it was just... Stranger Things,' Gaten Matarazzo told E! News. 'It was just everywhere. Like we'd just walk around and people would be talking about it.' In the same interview Millie Bobby Brown shared her own experience: 'I was at a Starbucks, and they didn't even ask my name. I was like, "oh by the way, my name's Millie", and they were like, "oh, we know".'

In a separate interview with ABC News, the cast revealed some more of their funny fan stories:

'I got followed back from my house by a couple in Toronto,' said Finn Wolfhard, who plays Mike Wheeler on the show. 'And the minute I got to my door, they were just like, "Can we take a picture with you?" I was like, "No, you followed me back for four blocks, that's super creepy."'

Millie Bobby Brown added that one time a girl sat down next to her while she was sleeping on a largely empty plane on the way to the Philippines. 'You know when you just, kind of, wake up and she's sitting right there? I'm like, "Hi",' she said. 'I just think that for me, because we're so young at the moment, it's like we haven't experienced this stuff yet, so for us it's like, "Whoa. That is just weird."'

Gaten Matarazzo, who plays Dustin Henderson, said some in the cast have even received marriage proposals: 'The marriage proposals are a little weird,' he commented.

Outside of us mere mortals the show has also attracted an army of celebrity followers. Comedian Amy Schumer revealed she was a fan by snapping a social media shot of her *Stranger Things*-inspired costume, while other A-listers including Reese Witherspoon, Octavia Spencer, Ryan Gosling, Emma Stone, Kevin Hart and Anna Kendrick have accosted the cast for selfies during awards ceremonies. *Breaking Bad* star Aaron Paul set the celebrity trend in motion. Speaking during an interview on the *Tonight Show with Jimmy Fallon*, the actor revealed he and his wife were huge fans of the show – so much so that he admitted to nerves before interviewing Millie Bobby Brown for *Elle* magazine, as part of a feature where celebrities interviewed other celebrities that they admire the most. 'I was terrified,' Paul told Fallon. 'She's the best ... but I was so terrified. She was on a family vacation [in] Spain, and I was like, "I've got to make this good." She gets on the phone with her cute little accent... She's far more articulate than I, and I was terrified.'

Harry Potter star Daniel Radcliffe, who knows a thing or two about finding fame at a young age, is another star who publicly geeked out over the *Stranger Things* crew. During a September 2016 interview on BBC Radio 1's Breakfast Show he went giddy about the fact that the actors would appear on the show the day after him. 'Oh my god,' Radcliffe said. 'OK, can you, like, just tell them that I think they're amazing and also just say, like, that as a person who started out acting really young, how are they so good? I wasn't that good when I was a kid. Have the decency to be less good at acting, please, when you're so young.'

Other celebrities took to social media to express their fandom, with the likes of Zac Efron and Hilary Duff posting their love for *Stranger Things*. Even Stephen King tweeted about the new international obsession. 'Watching STRANGER THINGS is looking watching Steve King's Greatest Hits,' he wrote in July 2016. 'I mean that in a good way.'

DIANE

The former wife of Chief Jim Hopper, Diane is played on the show by American actress Jerri Tubbs. We learn that Diane was married to Jim for seven years, during which time they had a daughter together, Sarah. In a flashback we see the happy family playing together in a park until Sarah begins to hyperventilate. Upon taking their daughter to the hospital we learn she has cancer. Later we see Diane watch on as her daughter dies.

We then discover that Diane has gone on to marry a man called Bill and had a second child. She is still in touch with Jim; he calls her for support as he struggles with the disappearance of Will Byers. Jim tells his ex-wife that he doesn't regret any of the seven years they had together, to which Diane asks if he has been drinking – insinuating that perhaps it was Hopper's struggles with alcohol that drove the two apart.

DUFFER BROTHERS

Born in February 1984, twin brothers Matt and Ross Duffer are the writers, directors and producers behind *Stranger Things*. Raised in Durham, North Carolina, the Duffers began making films when they were just eight or nine years old using a Sony Hi8 video camera that their parents had given to them as a gift. 'We just started filming anything and everything,' Matt Duffer said in an interview with North Carolina's *The News &*

Observer. 'And then, each summer, we made a feature-length movie. The first one was kind of unwatchable, but progressively, they got a little better and better.' That first attempt at a movie was apparently based on the popular card game Magic the Gathering. But while the result wasn't very good, by the brothers' own admission, they kept trying.

'We didn't have editing equipment, you know, we just were playing Danny Elfman music on a tape recorder,' Matt Duffer told radio station KPCC. 'But it was very fun and very creative, and that's what we did every summer. We refused to go to summer camp, so we just would wander around and make these movies.'

This love of filmmaking extended into their education when the brothers headed to Orange County, California to study at Chapman University Dodge College of Film and Media Arts. There, the brothers produced a series of short films to showcase their talents. One of the most notable was a film about an affluent family fleeing the plague in 1666 entitled *We All Fall Down*, which won Best Short at the 2005 Deep Ellum Film Festival in Dallas. Their thesis movie was entitled *Eater*, based on the Peter Crowther short story of the same name, and is a slick short that follows the story of a policeman working the night shift at a station when a cannibal prisoner breaks loose. The duo produced their thesis movie under the tutelage of *The Hunt for Red October* producer Mace Neufeld and the short later went on to be screened at festivals including Screamfest, the Santa Fe Film

Festival, Fantasy Filmfest, and the Bilbao International Festival of Documentary and Short Film.

After graduating in 2007 the pair struggled to get their big screenwriting break in Hollywood. During this time they continued to gain credits by writing and directing short films, but their breakthrough came with a spec script that they had written for the horror movie *Hidden*. The Duffers' script became the subject of a bidding war which was eventually won by Warner Bros. in 2011, who then asked the brothers to direct the picture. Principal photography started the following year in Vancouver with *True Blood* star Alexander Skarsgård in the leading role.

Hidden is an intriguing take on the age-old apocalypse genre. It follows a family of three who had sought shelter in an old bunker to avoid a viral outbreak that was turning people into monsters, but we then discover that the family have actually become infected, and that the monsters they were hiding from were not actually caused by the plague, but soldiers attempting to execute anyone who came into contact with it. The film received middling reviews and didn't make it to theatres, but speaking to *Entertainment Weekly*, the Duffers claimed the relative failure of their film spurred them on to greater things. 'Looking back on it, for us, it was using that low point as an advantage,' Ross said. 'I don't think *Stranger Things* would exist without it, because it was us being disillusioned with movies, the things we fell in love with, and then seeing this other opening in television that, if we really want to tell the kind of stories we want to tell, maybe we were just looking in the wrong place.'

One good thing to come out of *Hidden*, however, was that the movie caught the attention of acclaimed director M. Night Shyamalan who had read the Duffers' script and approached them to work on *Wayward Pines*, a science-fiction show he produced for Fox. The brothers are credited with writing three episodes from the show's first season including the fifth episode 'The Truth' which is widely regarded as the high watermark of the series. 'That became our training ground, and M. Night Shyamalan became a great mentor to us,' Ross Duffer told *Rolling Stone* about their experience on *Wayward Pines*. 'By the time we came out of that show, we were like, "OK, we know how to put together a show." And that's when we wrote *Stranger Things*.'

Using their newfound experience and contacts within the television industry the brothers began work on their own series, a mystery show called 'Montauk', a sci-fi series that attempts to uncover the mysterious disappearance of a young boy. It was this idea, as if you hadn't guessed yet, that would later be bought by Netflix and morph into *Stranger Things*.

The Duffers used their own love of pop culture, particularly their nostalgia for the 1980s, to inspire their own series. During their interview with North Carolina newspaper *The News & Observer*, Matt said: 'We have so much nostalgia and love for that era. I think we really wanted to see something on TV that was in the vein of the classic films we loved growing up – you know, the Steven Spielberg movies, John Carpenter films, Wes Craven films, Stephen King novels … Even though they're very tonally different – John Carpenter, obviously, is much darker than the types of films Steven Spielberg usually made – they all sort of explored the point where the ordinary meets the extraordinary.'

DUNGEONS & DRAGONS

Dungeons & Dragons (or D&D for short) is a fantasy role-playing board game that was first published in 1974. Designed by Gary Gygax and Dave Arneson it is one of the most popular games in the world, having been played by more than 20 million people and amassed sales of more than $1 billion.

In the game, each player takes on the role of a specific character. These characters range from wizards to warriors and dwarves to elves, each with their own equipment and abilities. As the characters complete quests, vanquish enemies in battle and find treasure they gain experience points that help them become increasingly powerful and take on a life of their own over a series of sessions.

The world of D&D is open-ended, with the action controlled by a single player who takes on the mantle of the Dungeon Master. The Dungeon Master serves as the game's referee as well as the fantasy world's principal storyteller. They develop and maintain the setting in which the action takes place and control the adversaries that the other players will face along the way. A good Dungeon Master is key to the game as they must be creative enough to devise and maintain an imaginary world for the other players to inhabit, while also having the ability to map out logical gameplay and recall hundreds of pages worth of rules. In *Stranger Things* Mike is shown as the crew's Dungeon Master, dictating the events that their fictional characters are faced with.

The other players have to navigate through this fantasy realm, engaging with the Dungeon Master to find out what fate befalls their hero. Random actions such as picking the lock to a door, negotiating an obstacle or attacking a foe require a dice roll with the score determining the outcome. In *Stranger Things* this action can be seen at the start of the season when Will attempts to cast a fireball in order to defeat the Demogorgon.

Dungeons & Dragons is a popular pastime of the boys in *Stranger Things*. Thanks to conversations within the show we learn that Mike, Dustin, Lucas and Will have been playing D&D since 1979 when they embarked on the Elder Tree campaign, with Mike's sister stepping in to play the role of the elf. Each of the boys has their own Dungeons & Dragons character. Will's wizard, Will the Wise, is the most talked about of these figures. However, through one of Will's drawings, we learn about the rest of the questing party which is formed of Dustin's dwarf,

Mike's Dungeon Master and Lucas's Knight – each of which feels like an appropriate choice of hero for the individual characters.

The boys' love of the game is shown in the opening episode when they are reaching the culmination of a ten-hour marathon D&D session, which ends with Mike summoning the Demogorgon and an army of troglodytes that defeats Will's character. In the show's final episode they are showing playing another quest on Christmas Eve with Mike summoning a Thessalhydra, another legendary D&D foe.

As well as signalling the boys' existence on the geekier end of the social spectrum, Dungeons & Dragons also plays an important referential role in explaining the events of *Stranger Things* with the game's figurines and board acting as props, as the show attempts to explain the more complex aspects of the Upside Down. Throughout the first season the boys use the game as a means of making sense of what is taking place. For example they choose to nickname the monster the Demogorgon, giving the otherwise nameless creature an identity. Later, Eleven also uses the game as an explanatory tool, flipping the board upside down to explain that Will is trapped in an alternate dimension, which they later nickname the Upside Down. She uses the Demogorgon figurine to explain that the monster was present within the Upside Down like Will was.

Dustin too uses the game to explain what the Upside Down is like, referencing the Vale of Shadows, describing it as a dimension that is a dark echo of the normal world, a place that is right next to you but you never see it.

Just as Dungeons & Dragons is used in the opening episode to foretell the events that would befall the boys during *Stranger Things*' first season, fans have speculated that the Christmas Eve game in the finale gives us a glimpse of what the future might hold for Will, Mike, Dustin and Lucas. Though they defeat the fearsome Thessalhydra, the boys' final quest features many unanswered questions. The boys list off unanswered loose ends such as a proud princess, a lost knight and strange flowers, all of which have clear counterparts in the dangling threads of the season one finale in the form of Eleven, Hopper and the Monster respectively. The final game also offers the Duffer Brothers an opportunity to poke fun at their audience. After the final battle Dustin asks 'That's not it, is it?' before Lucas adds, 'The campaign was way too short.' Both remarks can be seen as tongue-in-cheek comments from the show's creators directly to their audience.

Before *Stranger Things*, Dungeons & Dragons had featured in the universes of several TV shows such as *The Big Bang Theory*, *Community* and *Futurama*, and also in movies from *E.T.* (1982) to a *Dungeons & Dragons* film in 2000.

DYER, NATALIA

Natalia Dyer was born in Nashville, Tennessee on 13 January 1997. She began her acting career in community theatre where she played the character of Scout in a stage production of Harper Lee's novel *To Kill A Mockingbird*. The actress quite literally stumbled into acting. When she was younger her parents had signed her into a sports camp, but after straining her ankle on the first day she was forced to join an acting group instead, and instantly fell in love with the craft. She joined the Nashville School of the Arts and continued to perform in community theatre groups until graduating.

Natalia's first big role came in 2009 when she co-starred in *Hannah Montana: The Movie*. The actress played Clarissa, the daughter of the movie's conflicted villain, Oswald Granger, a British journalist who is intent on uncovering the double life of Hannah (played by Miley Cyrus). From there Natalia played a role in a string of minor movies including *The Greening of Whitney Brown* (2011) where she worked with stars including Brooke Shields, Kris Kristofferson, and Keith David.

Her first leading role, though, came in the 2014 indie flick *I Believe in Unicorns*. Written and directed by Leah Meyerhoff, the film tells the story of an awkward teenage girl who escapes into a fantasy world when her first romantic relationship turns increasingly violent. Natalia was just sixteen years old when she played the part of Davina, an imaginative, artistic and strong willed dreamer who is forced to grow up quickly as the sole carer of a terminally ill mother, and the girlfriend of an older lover who turns out to be anything but Prince Charming.

The film debuted at the 2014 SXSW festival and received largely positive reviews. According to the *Los Angeles Times*: 'A coming-of-age story about learning about love the hard way, *I Believe in Unicorns* feels like a teen movie made for an adult audience.' Dyer's performance in particular drew plaudits, with industry bible *Variety* describing her delicate portrayal of the film's central character as a 'Major Selling Point'. Movie website IndieWire went even further, calling her performance 'riveting', for a character that 'contains multitudes of contradictions: she seems fragile but demonstrates her strength, she's moody and also joyful, she's so painfully young and innocent but coming into her own as [a] woman.'

While living in New York and attending university, Dyer auditioned for *Stranger Things*. Speaking to *Harper's Bazaar* in September 2016 she revealed that, like much of the cast, she didn't know exactly what she was signing up for. 'The audition process was a fairly normal, fairly standard audition,' she said. 'I'm living in New York, and went in for the first audition and callbacks as well. It was mysterious. It was one of those things where you get sides [i.e. scenes] and you don't really get the script at first. You don't entirely know what's going on, so you just go in there to make your best guess as to what they're looking for. I do remember feeling not so good about either audition, coming out of them.'

Meanwhile, in *Cosmopolitan* magazine the actress revealed what drew her to the role: 'I do see a lot of roles that are, like, the girlfriend or the love interest or the girl next door. Maybe not totally well-rounded kinds of characters – women who are more of a plot device in a way. It was really nice to see a character like Nancy. She does have that love triangle and boy drama aspect to her, but she's independent and strong, and her main focus is about finding her best friend and solving that mystery at any cost. It's such a blessing to get to live in that role and bring that to life. And to be surrounded by other female characters while you're doing it! Having strong women who aren't damsels is so nice.'

Since appearing on *Stranger Things* Natalia's star has been on the rise in the entertainment business. The actress has become something of a style icon, appearing in photoshoots in magazines like *Vogue*. She has also been a mainstay of the gossip columns thanks to her rumoured romance with Charlie Heaton (who plays Jonathan Byers).

Shortly after the series landed on Netflix the couple became the subject of speculation as the world looked on, wanting to know if the two actors were doing what their characters couldn't do, and get together. The duo were snapped getting intimate at an airport in January 2017 and their Instagram profiles reveal that they spend a lot of downtime together, including a holiday in Spain in 2016. They were also spotted grabbing coffee together in Dyer's hometown of Nashville as rumours circulated that she had taken Charlie Heaton home to meet her family. From award-ceremony hangouts to off-set meet-ups the two of them appear to be inseparable. They even celebrated Halloween together in Atlanta, where they film the series, dressing as Wizard of Oz characters for the occasion.

The rumours of on-set romance delighted fans who had been fascinated by the Nancy-Steve-Jonathan love triangle from *Stranger Things*' first season. Indeed the hashtags #TeamSteve and #TeamJonathan were trending topics on social media for much of the summer of 2016, as fans sought to show where their loyalties lay regarding the show's teenage heartthrobs.

E

EGG

The egg is a mysterious item that can be spotted in the Upside Down throughout the show's first season. We initially see the egg in Eleven's first encounter with the Demogorgon when she is in the sensory deprivation tank. In a 'blink and you'll miss it' moment the Monster is shown hunched over eating the egg. The same sight is observed by Nancy when she falls through a portal to the Upside Down in the woods.

Finally audiences get an up-close look at the mysterious item during the first season's finale as Hopper investigates what appears to be a hollowed-out egg after passing through the gate into the Upside Down. The show is deliberately enigmatic about what the egg represents, but the most popular fan theory is that the egg is the Demogorgon's offspring, with many fans drawing parallels between the egg in *Stranger Things* and those found in Ridley Scott's 1979 smash hit *Alien,* one of the key cinematic influences on the Duffer Brothers.

EGGO

Eggo is a brand of frozen waffles produced by Kellogg's that first made it onto supermarket shelves in North America in the 1950s. Originally called Froffles, waffle fans started to call the product 'eggos' on account of the product's eggy taste. The name stuck and in 1955 the product officially underwent a name change.

The frozen breakfast food stuff is famous for its bright yellow packaging and available in all manner of flavours from wholegrain and buttermilk to cinnamon sugar and chocolate chip. Though they've been a fixture of the American diet for decades, Eggos enjoyed a resurgence in the USA and shot to worldwide fame after being featured in *Stranger Things*.

On the first series of *Stranger Things* the ready-made breakfast treat is the favourite food of telekinetic teenager Eleven. Our heroine is first introduced to the waffles by Mike, who is secretly housing the runaway government guinea pig in his basement. He brings Eleven a plateful of waffles to eat – probably because the freezer staple would have been plentiful in the Wheeler household, and also because the toaster-ready treats would have been easy for a young boy to prepare. Eleven quickly gets a taste for the treat and can later be found liberating a few boxes from the Hawkins location of Bradley's Big Buy. Obviously unaware of supermarket etiquette, shoppers stare on as Eleven stocks up on Eggos and heads for the exits, smashing the glass doors with her powers after being accosted by one of the clerks. In the next scene we see Eleven chomping down on the still-frozen snacks in the woods, and by the looks of it she's munching through her fourth box, which is an impressive twenty-four waffles in one sitting.

The humble Eggo also plays an important role in the series finale. At the conclusion of the episode Chief Hopper is shown taking some of the food from the station's Christmas party and leaving it in a box in the woods. Among the festive spread are Eggos, a short but significant hint to the audience that Eleven, who disappeared after her encounter with the Monster at Hawkins Middle School, might still be alive. It's one of the most iconic moments of the season finale, but amazingly the inclusion of the Eggos almost didn't happen. 'It was just going to be some food from the party,' producer Shawn Levy told *Business Insider*. 'The Duffers and I were talking about the scene over dinner one night and together we hatched this idea of leaving the Eggos specifically just to hint who he might be leaving the food for, or the hope of who he would be leaving the food for. That was one of 50 decisions that you stumble into and they become defining moments.'

Millie Bobby Brown apparently had to eat between 10 to 15 waffles per take while on set, even though she had a spit bucket to discard of her unwanted froffles, and the actress revealed at a panel at 2016's New York Comic Con that you can have too much of a good thing. When asked by a member of the audience what her true feelings towards Eggos were the actress answered: 'I like them, I do. But I do not like how many I eat. You see – the amount I eat is actually really hard to digest… [The waffle] does taste really nice but not like 15 times in a row. I do like the blueberry flavour.'

Eggos are to *Stranger Things* what Reese's Pieces are to *E.T.*, a piece of period-friendly product placement that also happens to be an important plot device. Like *E.T.*'s influence on the sale of chocolate-coated peanut candy (sales increase: 300 per cent in the wake of the movie's release) Kellogg's saw sales of Eggos soar in the wake of *Stranger Things*' release. The brand became heavily involved on social media, taking any opportunity to draw a line between the show and their products.

The company was even involved in the promotion of *Stranger Things*' second season, particularly the TV spot that aired during the 2017 Super Bowl to tease the show's return to Netflix. The trailer, which gave audiences their first glimpse at the show's second season, began with a vintage Eggo advert from 1980 that then gives way to an image of Eleven with blood pouring from her nose. Eggo's involvement in the ad made them one of the big winners from the annual American Football finale, which is one of the world's most watched events. According to researchers the trailer generated more than 307,000 tweets during the game, which was more than three times that of any other brand.

ELEVEN

Eleven, played by Millie Bobby Brown, is one of the central characters in *Stranger Things*. A twelve-year-old girl with a shaved head and psychic abilities, Eleven – or El as she is known to Mike and his friends – was born in the early 1970s. Originally called Jane, Eleven is the daughter of Terry Ives, a test subject in the Project MKUltra experiments, although she was abducted from her mother shortly after her birth. After that she was raised in the Hawkins Laboratory under the guidance of Dr Brenner whom she refers to as 'Papa'.

During her time in the Hawkins Laboratory, Eleven was kept in a sparse subterranean cell and forced to partake in a number of experiments. During one we see her crush a Coke can with her telekinetic powers; during another she repeats what an employee in another room is saying over the lab's loudspeakers. Two other experiments, however, show just how powerful her abilities are. After she is presented with a cat that she refuses to kill with her telekinetic powers, Eleven is forcibly dragged away to her cell by two guards who she kills in anger. Later, using the help of a sensory deprivation tank she is able to eavesdrop on the conversation of a Russian operative over a great distance. Throughout the series we see examples of Eleven's powers, from contacting the Upside Down through radio equipment to levitating Mike at the quarry, and she even flings a transit van into the air in order to help her and her friends evade capture from the bad men. In 2016's season one finale we also see the offensive extent of her powers as she faces off against a small army of Hawkins Laboratory agents before finally going to toe-to-tendril with the Demogorgon.

Though we never see the origin of Eleven's powers, or their full extent, we do know that they take a physical toll on the young girl. After each use of her abilities, she is shown to suffer from a nosebleed, a sign of the physical effects of her abilities, and from exhaustion due to over-exerting herself. The mental scars of her time in captivity at Hawkins Laboratory are also evident in her personality. Presumably deprived of social interaction for much of her life, she is timid and nervous around people. Her adolescent isolation has also led her to have extremely limited social skills. A girl of very few words, she can struggle to make her feelings and thoughts understood to the other characters in *Stranger Things* and relies on Mike and his friends to help her survive and adjust to the world outside of the laboratory. It seems her time spent as Dr Brenner's guinea pig has also scarred her psychologically. Her time in the sensory deprivation tanks has resulted in extreme claustrophobia, and she has frequent outbursts of anger. However she is also shown to be fiercely loyal to her new friends, coming to their rescue on multiple occasions.

As one of the show's primary characters we're first introduced to Eleven during the very first episode when she sneaks into Benny's diner and starts to steal fries. After having a meal cooked for her by the soon-to-be-deceased diner owner, we get a glimpse of the twelve-year-old's voracious appetite which would later see her scoff Eggos at an alarming rate. It's the lighter side of a character who has undoubtedly been subjected to some of the harshest treatment in the series so far.

After escaping Agent Connie Frazier and the 'bad men' of the Hawkins Laboratory, Eleven bumps into Mike and his friends. The chance encounter is the beginning of a friendship that would blossom over the series: the boys help to teach El about everyday life while she helps them on their quest to find their lost friend Will. It is El who helps to educate the boys on the Upside Down, and she also helps them to contact Will, defeat their school bullies and ultimately saves them from the Demogorgon. But she is also helped: Mike takes El into his home, feeding her, clothing her and teaching her the basics of friendship. A burgeoning romance is also blossoming between the two by the end of the series when Mike asks El to the Snow Ball school dance.

During the first season finale it seems like El makes the ultimate sacrifice as she rescues the boys from the Demogorgon, but a final scene in which Chief Hopper leaves a box of Eggos in the woods suggests that the heroine is still very much alive. Indeed not long after a second season was confirmed it was announced that Millie Bobby Brown would also reprise her role as the shaven-headed psychic.

The Duffer Brothers have said that the inspiration behind Eleven's character came from the MKUltra experiments, but there are obvious similarities, too, between her relationship with Mike and the dynamic at the heart of Steven Spielberg's *E.T.* But the Duffers have also cited *Elfen Lied*, *Akira,* and *Silent Hill* as elements that make up Eleven's onscreen DNA.

ELFEN LIED

Elfen Lied is a Japanese manga series that ran from 2002 to 2005. It was also adapted for TV in 2004. The stories revolve around the differences between humans and beings called Dicloni, a species of mutants who are similar to humans but who have horns and telekinetic powers. The main human character was a teenage girl who wants to exact revenge on the humans who wouldn't accept her, while the themes included alienation, acceptance, and humanity. The Duffer Brothers have previously cited this series as a primary influence on the character of Eleven.

THE EMPIRE STRIKES BACK (1980)

Released three years before when *Stranger Things* is set, *The Empire Strikes Back* was a worldwide sensation, so it is safe to assume that George Lucas's *Star Wars* sequel would have been among Mike, Will, Lucas and Dustin's favourite films. Indeed, there is evidence in the show itself: Mike introduces Eleven to toys via his Yoda action figure and later describes her telekinetic powers as 'Jedi-like'. Lucas also uses *Star Wars* as a reference point, referring to Eleven as 'Lando' – referring to Billy Dee Williams' character of Lando Calrissian – when he believes she has betrayed them.

EPISODES

Following *Stranger Things'* first season of eight episodes, which debuted on Netflix in July 2016, a second run of nine episodes were scheduled to air from 27 October 2017, making seventeen in all. Each episode title is a numbered chapter, with a subtitle that cleverly hints at the action to come. After realising that season one's chapter titles contained cryptic clues, fans were whipped up into a frenzy of excitement when, in late 2016, the Duffer Brothers decided to unveil the episodic titles well in advance of the show's second season. Soon the internet was awash with videos, articles and discussions about what the titles might mean and fan theories about the action we might see unfold in season two.

It turns out that some of those fan theories were correct to such an extent that the show's creative team decided to deliberately withhold some of the final chapter titles for fear of giving away spoilers. 'Some of them are changing,' Matt Duffer admitted to *Entertainment Weekly*. 'Some of them we didn't put because these people are smart on the f—ing internet. You've seen it with *Westworld* — they figured it out! I've seen videos analyzing the chapter titles and they're right on a lot.'

The brothers shared similar sentiments in another interview with the *Hollywood Reporter*. 'Even if they aren't the final chapter titles, everything in that teaser is major,' Matt Duffer said. 'But they're ambiguous enough that no one is going to be able to figure it out. Some of the fan theories online are amazing. Most are wrong, but I've read a few that are right or very close. Is it Reddit? Some of those people have figured stuff out based off of the chapter titles.'

As with seemingly everything else in *Stranger Things*, the chapter titles for the show's first and second seasons are crammed full of pop culture references. For example, 'Chapter Two: The Weirdo on Maple Street' in season one is a clever reference to an episode of *The Twilight Zone*, a creeptastic American anthology series that originally ran from 1959 to 1964 and was later revived in the late 1980s and early 2000s. Originally airing on 4 March 1960, 'The Monsters Are Due on Maple Street' is one of the show's most loved episodes and centres on a sleepy suburban street that descends into paranoia at the prospect of an alien invasion. Episode four's title 'The Body', meanwhile, is a reference to a Stephen King novella that was later adapted for the hit movie *Stand by Me*.

The title of Stranger Things' second season opening episode nods at further pop culture references. 'Chapter One: Madmax' alludes to the infamous post-apocalyptic character of the same name from George Miller's iconic Road Warrior movies. Both *Mad Max* (1979) and *Mad Max 2: The Road Warrior* (1981) would have been released before the events that unfold in Hawkins, so could well have influenced *Stranger Things*' characters just as other movies such as *Star Wars*, *E.T.,* and *Jaws* have done.

E.T.: THE EXTRA TERRESTRIAL (1982)

The motherlode of *Stranger Things* movie references. If you had to choose one film that had a profound impact on the Duffer Brothers' creation of their smash hit show it would be this Steven Spielberg classic. Originally released in 1982, the film tells the story of Elliott, a lonely boy who befriends a stranded extra-terrestrial before he and his siblings help it return home while attempting to keep it hidden from their mother and the government. Based on an imaginary friend Spielberg had created following his parents' divorce, *E.T.* was a critical and commercial success story. It was nominated for nine Oscars (it won four), took $800 million at the box office and helped to shape cinema as we know it today. In fact the movie's impact was so profound that after beating *E.T.* to the Oscar for Best Picture at the 55th Academy Awards, *Gandhi* director Richard

Attenborough said: 'I was certain that not only would *E.T.* win, but that it should win. It was inventive, powerful, [and] wonderful. I make more mundane movies.'

There's no doubt that *Stranger Things* is a love letter to Spielberg's iconic 1980s movie. Just look at the central premise, wherein bike-pedalling kids from a sleepy American suburb are hounded by government agents after they discover an otherworldly being. Sound familiar?

There are other reference points too. Winona Ryder clearly channels *E.T.*'s Dee Wallace as a single mother trying to make ends meet whilst bringing up her children. While there's no Speak & Spell in sight, the crew's use of walkie talkies to contact the Upside Down is reminiscent of the MacGyvering in Spielberg's classic movie, and finally Eleven's love of Eggos is nothing but a nod in the direction of the little grey man's penchant for Reese's Pieces.

Perhaps the most obvious moment of inspiration, though, comes in the form of the bicycle chase from the show's first season. In Chapter Seven, Mike and the gang are helping Eleven to escape from the shadowy figures of the Hawkins Laboratory in a thrilling pedal-powered chase through the streets of Hawkins. The sequence is almost a scene-for-scene remake of *E.T.*'s iconic chase scene, but instead of levitating the bikes out of harm's way like the titular alien, Eleven uses her supernatural powers to flip one of the vans that's attempting to chase them down.

THE EVIL DEAD (1981)

Sam Raimi's cult classic is infamous as one of the original 'video nasties' of the 1980s. One of the most gruesome films of its era, it was one of the first horror movies to be X-rated upon its release and so only really found fame after it was made available on home video. In *Stranger Things* Jonathan Byers has a poster for the movie on his bedroom wall, which his deadbeat dad tells him to take down in episode five as it is 'inappropriate'. *The Evil Dead* has no doubt also influenced some of the visuals in *Stranger Things*, and there is an eerie establishing shot of the Byers' house in episode one in particular that is reminiscent of Raimi's movie.

FAKE BODY

In an effort to cover up his disappearance as a result of their experiments, Hawkins Laboratory mocks up a fake body of Will Byers. The body is found in the quarry during the fourth episode of the first season (which takes its name from the copycat corpse). Hawkins instructs State Trooper David O'Bannon to discover the body, which later would arouse the suspicion of Chief Hopper as would the choice of coroner as the laboratory hires out of town agents to take the body to the morgue instead of the usual attendants.

Chief Hopper isn't the only person to have suspicious over the cadaver, though. It is Joyce Byers who first questions whether it is actually Will as he had made contact with her from the Upside Down. Even upon seeing his body, when she is called in to identify it, Joyce refuses to believe that Will is dead as the body does not have the birthmark that her son has. Eventually Hopper begins to accept her suspicions. He breaks into the morgue and uses his knife to cut into the body, only to discover it was a fake stuffed with cotton wool.

FAKE TRAILER

While developing *Stranger Things* the Duffer Brothers put together a 'fake trailer' for the show to give the networks a feel for the look and tone of the series. The trailer was mocked up from some of the movies that inspired the brothers and which would later be referenced in the show's first season. The trailer was made up of a total of twenty-five clips from movies such as *E.T.*, *Nightmare on Elm Street*, and *Poltergeist*, set to the score from John Carpenter's *The Fog*.

FAN FICTION

Like just about every modern-day pop culture phenomenon *Stranger Things* has spawned its own curious breed of fan fiction. A cursory search online will reveal all manner of hare-brained scribblings ranging from Mike and El love stories, saucy tales of Nancy and Jonathan's sexual exploits and even a bizarre story in which the cast of *Harry Potter* interact with the *Stranger Things* crew in Hawkins.

One of the most famous examples of *Stranger Things* fan fiction, however, imagined that El grew up to become the central figure from *Legally Blonde*, presumably because she shares the same name as Reese Witherspoon's character. The story was published by Australian writer Kaitlyn Plyley on her blog and imagined the challenges Eleven would face growing up in the Valley, hiding her powers under layers of pink and studying for her degree at Harvard. 'Elle surrounded herself with soft, pink things – fluffy pillows, sweet fragrances – and avoided anything that would make her seem intimidating,' Plyley writes. 'It took her a long time to work out that she was still trying to prove she wasn't the monster.'

The blog post was shared across the web and was picked up by established media outlets. The same idea was shared by many readers on social media who began to mash up stills from the movie with El taking the place of the sorority girl turned star lawyer who made the film famous.

FILMING LOCATIONS

Although it is set in the fictional town of Hawkins, Indiana, *Stranger Things* was actually shot on location in the state of Georgia. However Georgia wasn't the first location that had been proposed for filming. The Duffer Brothers had originally wanted to shoot around Long Island near New York as they had envisaged setting the show against the backdrop of a small coastal town. It turned out, though, that a winter shoot in Long Island wasn't possible for both financial and meteorological reasons and so the production was moved south.

'We're actually from North Carolina, so when we wound up in Atlanta and I started scouting Atlanta we got excited about it, because it looked actually much more like our own childhoods,' Matt Duffer told the *Hollywood Reporter* in 2016. 'It reminded me of my own childhood. I don't know what it's like to live on a coast, so it was actually once we settled into it and got used to the idea and we came up with this town name, Hawkins.'

The town of Jackson, located about fifty miles outside of Atlanta, served as the backdrop for downtown Hawkins, whilst many of the interior sets were built and filmed on sound stages in EUE Screen Gems Studios.

'THE FLEA AND THE ACROBAT'

'The Flea and the Acrobat' is the name of the fifth episode of *Stranger Things*' first season. The episode is written by Alison Tatlock and directed by the Duffer Brothers. The action centres on the apparent funeral of Will Byers, but the principal characters no longer believe that the body inside the coffin is real. Indeed, during the wake, the boys are more interested in quizzing Mr Clarke about the physics of alternate dimensions than dealing with their friend's death.

Meanwhile Jonathan and Nancy plan to attack and kill the Monster captured in Jonathan's photo. To that end they set off in search of the Monster in the wood, armed with Lonnie's pistol and an arsenal of other assorted weaponry. As they explore the woods they come across a wounded deer, but just as they get ready to put the animal out of its misery the Demogorgon drags it away. Following the trail of blood Nancy gets sucked into the Upside Down through a portal beneath the tree.

Elsewhere in this episode trouble begins to brew between the boys as Lucas starts to suspect Eleven, and the telekinetic girl accidentally knocks Mike's best friend unconscious during a squabble.

THE FOG (1980)

As well as using the score from John Carpenter's thriller for the Duffers' *Stranger Things* fake trailer, the brothers were also heavily influenced by the film itself when creating their show's first season. *The Fog* tells the story of a radio DJ who inadvertently broadcast a century-old message that puts his small community in danger from the ghosts of ancient mariners. The use of the ham radio in *Stranger Things* to access the Upside Down echoes the use of the radio station in *The Fog* to access the spirits of sailors.

FRAZIER, CONNIE

Played by Catherine Dyer, Connie Frazier is a recurring character during *Stranger Things*' first season. A colleague of Dr Brenner's at the sinister Hawkins Laboratory, Frazier is the henchwoman of choice for the clandestine organization.

It is Agent Frazier who intercepts Benny Hammond's phone call about a shaven-headed girl visiting his diner, and after posing as a member of social services it is she who kills the diner owner and later frames his death as a suicide. She also visits Mr Clarke in a bid to locate Eleven and later tracks her, alongside the boys, to Hawkins Middle School. After holding the kids at gunpoint Eleven uses her powers to make Connie bleed through her eyes and the character drops down dead.

Speaking during a Reddit AMA Catherine Dyer summed up what made her character such an important part of the show. 'I loved the shock of Connie shooting Benny,' she said. 'I feel that scene really set the tone for the show. No one knew what to expect. And yes, every time Connie came to the door you didn't know what to expect!' Indeed, Agent Frazier was the villain you loved to hate and a more hands-on threat than the altogether more cerebral figure of Dr Brenner.

FUNERAL

After Will Byers' body is apparently discovered in the Hawkins quarry, his funeral takes place on 11 November 1983 with Will's friends and family present. Will is buried in the casket Jonathan picked out for him. When the ceremony is over, Jonathan and Nancy decide to track down and kill the Monster whilst Mike and the gang get an explanation in alternate dimensions from Mr Clarke.

G

THE GOONIES (1985)

With the exception of *E.T.: The Extra Terrestrial*, the movie to which *Stranger Things* perhaps owes the greatest debt is the 1985 cult classic, *The Goonies*. Directed by Richard Donner and produced by one of the Duffer Brothers' favourite directors, Steven Spielberg, the film tells the story of a group of nerdy teens who embark on an adventure without the knowledge of their parents. If that sounds familiar it's because this exact same spirit imbues the Netflix series, but the stakes are a little higher and the goings-on are slightly spookier when dealing with a clandestine government agency and a monstrous entity from another dimension rather than One Eyed Willie's 17th Century treasure map.

THE GATE

The Gate, also referred to as the rift, is a portal to the Upside Down that is located in a sub basement of the Hawkins National Laboratory facility. Though temporary portals open up throughout the town of Hawkins, the Gate is the only permanent bridge between the two dimensions of *Stranger Things*.

The Gate was created after Eleven came into contact with the Monster in the Upside Down. Placed in a sensory deprivation tank to enhance her psychic abilities, the telekinetic was encouraged by Dr Brenner to reach out to the being, and upon touching it she caused a rift between the two dimensions that cracked open the wall of the tank room. The Gate enabled the Monster to escape the Upside Down, causing panic in the Hawkins Laboratory, and the ensuing chaos enabled Eleven to escape her captors.

After the incident the area was immediately contained and placed under quarantine, which we see at the very beginning of the show with the blast doors to the subterranean basement being sealed off, and later Dr Brenner and his team returned to the gate to study the portal and its effects. Wearing hazmat suits Dr Brenner and his team sent Shepard, a Hawkins Laboratory employee, to investigate what was beyond the Gate.

Later in the series Chief Hopper becomes the first outsider to learn of the Gate's existence after he breaks into Hawkins Laboratory in search of Will Byers. Though he is knocked unconscious and removed by the lab's security team, he returns to the Gate during the series finale when he and Joyce enter the portal in order to find and retrieve Will. As far as we can tell from the first season, Shepard, Hopper and Joyce are the only people to have entered the Upside Down via the Gate.

Unlike the temporary rifts that exist between Hawkins and the Upside Down, the Gate provides a permanent connection to the other dimension. As a result the Upside Down has started to bleed into the Hawkins Laboratory, infecting the former deprivation tank room with the same airborne spores that are prevalent on the other side of the portal. The Gate itself shows signs that the Upside Down is spreading across the divide. Growing out of it are also the same root-like tendrils that cover everything on the other side. It also has a slimy texture, and pulses and gargles as if the Gate itself is alive.

GARY

Played by Mark Withers in a minor role during *Stranger Things'* first season, Gary (whose last name is never mentioned) is the coroner of the local morgue. Chief Hopper calls him to the police station in order to question him about the autopsy of Will Byers' body. Gary tells Hopper that he was surprised that Byers' body was accompanied by so much security and that the State Police claimed jurisdiction despite the body being found at the Hawkins quarry. This testimony fuels the Chief's suspicions, prompting Hopper to break into the morgue and discover that Will's body was in fact a fake.

GREENBERG, RICHARD

Richard Greenberg is a visual effects artist who is renowned for his work for some of Tinseltown's most famous movies. Greenberg's CV reads like a checklist of influential films, including the likes of *Predator*, *Last Action Hero* and *Flash Gordon*. Some of Greenberg's most memorable work however includes the production of title sequences for a trio of terrific movies in *Superman*, *Alien* and *The Dead Zone*; or, to put it another way, 'Pretty much every awesome title sequence back in the day,' as Ross Duffer noted in an interview with pop culture website the A.V. Club.

Greenberg's visual effects work inspired the Duffers when deciding on their series title sequence design. Ross Duffer told the A.V. Club: 'It's something very very simple, but very very memorable. Like *Alien*, just those little lines forming. That is so effective and so memorable, but is something that is so ridiculously simple.'

H

H, TOMMY

The freckled friend of Steve Harrington, the recurring character of Tommy H, played by Chester Rushing, is a student of Hawkins High School, where he spends most of his time hanging out with Steve, Nancy and Carol.

Tommy is Carol's boyfriend, and according to Barb the two have been 'having sex since, like, seventh grade'. Less is known about the seventeen-year-old's relationship with Steve, though we can safely assume that they're pretty close as Tommy attended the party at Steve's house on the night of Barb's disappearance.

Portrayed as a typical high school bully Tommy is something of a pantomime villain in *Stranger Things*' first season. Whether he's mocking Nancy's surprise that Steve would be hosting a party on a school night, or claiming to not remember who Barb is, he is callously cruel at any and every opportunity. One of his more appalling moments comes after it is revealed that Jonathan Byers was taking photos of the group on the night of Steve's party. Confronting the amateur photographer and sometime peeping tom in the school parking lot, Tommy takes great pleasure in smashing his victim's camera to smithereens.

His cruelty continues – he helps Steve daub offensive graffiti on the front of Hawkins' town cinema when his bequiffed friend mistakenly thinks that Nancy is cheating on him with Jonathan. He later goads his friend into fighting the elder Byers boy in a Hawkins alleyway, an altercation that eventually leads the four teens to be arrested. It is this incident that seemingly spells the beginning of the end of Tommy's friendship with Steve.

Despite what viewers might have wished, Tommy somehow escapes the clutches of the Demogorgon during *Stranger Things*' first season, although if he maintains that same level of douchery in future episodes, we can only hope that he gets his eventual comeuppance.

HAMMOND, BENNY

Played by Chris Sullivan, Benny Hammond is the owner and chef at Benny's Diner in Hawkins. Benny is the first person that Eleven meets after escaping from the lab and the big man is shown to have a big heart as he takes her in, clothing and feeding her before calling social services to find her somewhere safe to stay.

Benny is shown to be one of the good guys, popular with locals who dine at his establishment and friends with just about everyone in town apart from a few ex-girlfriends who 'didn't like him much'. Unfortunately his brief encounter with Eleven ultimately leads to his demise after Hawkins Laboratory intercepts his call to social services and sends Agent Frazier to murder Benny, posing the scene as a suicide to throw off suspicion.

HARBOUR, DAVID

Born on 10 April 1974, David Harbour plays the regular character of Chief Jim Hopper on *Stranger Things*. Born in New York, Harbour attended Byram Hills High School in Armonk. Though he didn't know it, high school would represent Harbour's first brush with Hollywood as two of his contemporaries, Sean Maher and Eyal Podell, would later go on to become actors. Harbour got his big break in 1999 when he appeared in the Broadway revival of N. Richard Nash's play *The Rainmaker*. That same year he made his TV debut in an episode of the long-running *Law & Order*, a show which he would return to a further four times, most recently in 2009. Harbour has also made guest appearances in episodes of popular network shows such as *Elementary* and *Lie to Me*.

Despite his sporadic guest appearances on the small screen, Harbour's best work on the idiot box has come when he's been given the opportunity to play a recurring character. He was excellent as an MI6 agent for six episodes of *Mad Men* wannabe *Pan-Am*, and one of the stand-out stars of NBC's short lived espionage drama *State of Affairs*. He also played a TV anchor on Aaron Sorkin's *The Newsroom* between 2012 and 2014.

During nearly two decades on the small screen, Harbour also spent some time in Hollywood working on films ranging from *Revolutionary Road* to *Suicide Squad* via a brush with Bond in *Quantum of Solace*. His silver screen resume echoes his TV work in that his career has seen him play everything from walk on roles to bit part characters. However, perhaps his stand-out cinematic performance came in Ang Lee's *Brokeback Mountain*.

His many onscreen appearances, though, had never quite led to that all-important breakthrough. 'I've really done so much work and no one's cared,' Harbour told host Ophira Eisenberg on NPR's *20-Sided Quiz* podcast. But in 2015 he landed the role that would finally turn him into a household name.

'I had done a show for NBC that just got cancelled. And I talked to my television agent and she asked, what would you be interested in doing? And I was like, I would love to play a broken, flawed, antihero character,' Harbour said in an interview with *The Daily Beast* in August 2016 explaining what had drawn him to the *Stranger Things* script. 'It was the best pilot script I'd ever read…It was the guy I've always wanted to play and

I thought, well, I'll never get cast in this, so I may as well read it and enjoy it, but I'm sure they're going to want a big star for this, because it's a real flashy role.'

Harbour couldn't have been more mistaken. The Duffer brothers thought that the actor would be the perfect choice to play Chief Hopper on *Stranger Things* and the rest, as they say, is history. 'David is just someone who I think has been waiting too long for this opportunity,' Matt Duffer told the same website. 'He is such an amazing actor and he just hasn't been given the platform, that's all. So it was exciting for us to go, OK well let's give it to this guy. We knew he was gonna knock it out of the park. I love him so much. He's such a badass.'

As one of the standout stars of the first season of *Stranger Things*, Harbour's performance landed him both critical acclaim and awards success with nominations for Best Supporting TV Actor at the 2017 Fangoria Chainsaw Awards. Harbour also became a star on the awards circuit, becoming a prominent figure as the ensemble cast walked the red carpet. He hit the headlines in 2016 after the same cast won the gong for Outstanding Performance by an Ensemble Cast at the Screen Actors Guild Awards. It was there that Harbour delivered his politically-charged acceptance speech criticising President Donald Trump's new administration.

With his star on the rise following his appearance on *Stranger Things,* Harbour was cast opposite Jamie Foxx on Baran bo Odar's Las Vegas cop caper *Sleepless*. He has also been heavily linked with a slew of other silver screen roles including a possible appearance in the comic book movie *Deadpool 2*. As well as his work on the big screen Harbour also enjoyed some time on stage, where he has continued to perform since his 1999 Broadway debut. Indeed he was supposed to play the character of Achilles in the Public Theater's production of Shakespeare's *Troilus and Cressida* in the summer of 2016, but was forced to withdraw after literally snapping his achilles tendon on stage, an injury that required him to recuperate after surgery.

HARRINGTON, STEVE

Played by Joe Keery, recurring character Steve Harrington is one of the cool kids at Hawkins High School, and is the owner of some of the best hair to ever grace the small screen. Steve dresses well, drives an imported car, drinks beer, and hosts parties by his pool when his parents are out of town. In many ways he is the prototypical eighties heartthrob, so it's perhaps not a shock that he's had a string of relationships or that Nancy Wheeler has such a big crush on him.

In a show that often celebrates nerdery, it should come as no surprise that Steve is initially something of a villain. He's best friends with Tommy H and Carol, two of the more unlikeable residents of Hawkins. His intentions towards Nancy are also anything but wholesome, and later he plays a part in destroying Jonathan's camera after finding out that he had been taking photos of his encounter with Nancy at the party. In fact towards the end of the series he lurches into full-blown villain mode, first daubing offensive graffiti about Nancy on the Hawkins cinema sign and later engaging in a bout of fisticuffs with Jonathan.

However, in the final two episodes of the first season Steve undergoes something of a redemption. He experiences an epiphany while waiting for Tommy to buy him a soda at a petrol station. He calls his former friends 'assholes' and sets out to atone for his actions, first cleaning the graffiti he scrawled on the local cinema, and then attempting to apologise to Jonathan and Nancy. His timing couldn't be worse, though – he does not realise that Jonathan and Nancy are by now on a mission to kill the Demogorgon. When he shows up at the Byers' house, he becomes entangled in the plot to catch and kill the beast, rushing to Nancy's aid by clubbing the Monster with a baseball bat. He ends the first season clad in a colourful Christmas sweater and snuggling with Nancy on the sofa. Not only has the former bequiffed bad boy got the girl, it seems like he's also buried the hatchet with Jonathan after gifting his one-time adversary with a new camera in honour of the festive season.

The events of the first season have made an enduring impact on Steve. He evolves from unlikeable cool kid to a genuinely compassionate character. According to an interview they conducted with *Variety,* the Duffer Brothers had originally intended Steve to be 'the biggest douchebag on the planet', but during development of the series they decided to expand the character's role. 'A lot of credit goes to Joe Keery [who plays Steve], because he was much more likeable and charming than we originally had envisioned,' said Ross Duffer. 'Joe was so good we started to fall in love with the idea that he has an arc himself.'

Steve turned out to be one of the most popular characters with fans of the show, so much so that he was the subject of an absurd theory that started to gain traction online through social media. The theory suggested that Steve was the father of another popular TV character with big hair, *Parks and Recreation*'s Jean-Ralphio Saperstein (Ben Schwartz). Seemingly the only proof of that pop culture connection, though, was that both characters hail from Indiana, and that Jean-Ralphio was born in 1985 – two years after the events of *Stranger Things* took place – so the timeline kind of fits. Nevertheless when Joe Keery and Ben Schwartz appeared together on an episode of James Corden's *The Late Late Show,* they made fans' dreams come true by performing a father/son skit that jokingly supported the outlandish theory.

HAWKINS

Located in Roane County in Indiana, Hawkins is the fictional setting for *Stranger Things*. A sleepy town with a small centre and a sprawl of suburban homes, it is the epitome of Middle America, and the same kind of white-picket fenced backdrop that's been a staple of TV and movies over the years.

Not much is known about the history of Hawkins. Early on we're told the last person to go missing in the town was in 1923, a full 60 years prior to the events of *Stranger Things*, so we can surmise that the town is relatively incident-free, something that seems to be reinforced by the police department's 'relaxed' approach to law enforcement. The main employers in the town seem to be the local quarry and the Hawkins National Laboratory. The downtown area is also home to a smattering of local businesses including Melvald's General Store, RadioShack, Bradley's Big Buy and the Royal Furniture Co. as well as local government institutions ranging from a Public Library and schools, to the Roane County Morgue and Hawkins Water & Sewage Authority.

Hawkins is surrounded by woodland, most prominently the area Will and his friends know as Mirkwood which is located to the south of the town, and which divides the urban area from the fenced-off facilities of the National Laboratory. Judging by the map which Jonathan takes from the Hawkins phonebook to track the locations of the Monster's attacks, Hawkins itself is relatively small. The urban area is roughly three times the size of the Mirkwood, and only has a handful of major roads, showing us that Hawkins is anything but a metropolis even if it is large enough to house two schools, a police department and a general hospital.

HAWKINS NATIONAL LABORATORY

A fictional extension of the US Department of Energy, this malevolent facility is located in a remote, forested area with a single road providing it with access to the rest of the town of Hawkins.

Though it poses as a Department of Energy institution the complex is no doubt controlled by the CIA, NSA or some other clandestine government agency, a point that is proved emphatically by the 'Bad Men' who man it, and the experiments they conduct there. Though it is never overtly stated, we can surmise that it is here that Dr Brenner originally conducted his MKUltra experiments following World War II. The continued use of the facility to explore the extent of Eleven's psychic powers shows that it continues to be a site for shady dealings in the *Stranger Things* context of 1983.

As you might imagine for a secretive government black site, the Hawkins National Laboratory complex is heavily protected. Ringed with fences, barbed wire, and military personnel, it is more of a fortress than a scientific facility. The same is true of the interior which is filled with subterranean basements that house prison cells, sensory deprivation tanks, and interrogation rooms.

The lab itself is at the centre of much of the action in *Stranger Things*' first season. It is epicentre of the Upside Down, the place where the Gate is formed, where the Monster first breaks through, and where eventually

Will Byers is rescued after Hopper and Joyce Byers break in to enter the alternate dimension and save him.

HAWKINS HIGH SCHOOL

One of Hawkins' two schools, Hawkins High is attended by Jonathan, Barb, Nancy, Tommy, and Carol. The school football team is known as the Tigers, corresponding with the Cubs of the town's middle school, and it is on their field that an assembly is held following Will Byers' disappearance. During the first season we briefly see the school's principal (played by Salem Murphy) when she appears to call Nancy out of a lesson. The real life Patrick Henry High School in Stockbridge, Georgia was used as the backdrop for the school scenes in season one of *Stranger Things*.

HAWKINS MIDDLE SCHOOL

Located next door to the town's High School, Hawkins Middle School is where Mike, Dustin, Lucas and Will receive their education. The school has a gymnasium in which an assembly is held following Will's apparent death. It is here that Eleven uses her powers to make Troy wet himself and where the *Stranger Things* squad create a make-shift sensory deprivation tank in order to locate Will in the Upside Down. During the finale of season one of the show, Hawkins Middle School is the scene of a climactic fight between the Demogorgon,

Eleven and the 'Bad Men' from Hawkins National Laboratory.

As well as a burgeoning A.V. Club which boasts top of the range radio equipment, Hawkins Middle School is also home to a football team (The Cubs) and Mr Clarke who is one of the most gifted teachers in Roane County.

THE HAWK

The Hawk is a local cinema located in downtown Hawkins. We know that it shows most of the era's big releases, as Joyce Byers reveals that she snuck her son Will into The Hawk to watch *Poltergeist* upon its release. During the events of *Stranger Things* the Hawk is screening 1983's *All the Right Moves*, a high school football film that helped to make Tom Cruise a star, and which according to Steve's derogatory graffiti, also features 'Nancy the Slut Wheeler'.

HAYES, JENNIFER

Jennifer Hayes is a student from Hawkins Middle School who attends Will Byers' funeral. Dustin spots her crying during the service, leading him to believe that she had a crush on Will, ;something that he delights in telling his friend when he returns from the Upside Down.

HEATHKIT HAM RADIO

This brand of educational electronic equipment is mentioned by name by Mr Clarke when he calls the boys in for an impromptu meeting of the school A.V. Club. Heathkits were produced by the Heath Company, the most prominent manufacturers of educational radio equipment at the time. In business from 1942 to 2014, the Heath Company produced everything from basic oscilloscopes to more complex radio kits. They were immensely popular tools for educating children about electronics due to their cost effective nature and ease of assembly, and are said to have been one of the earliest inspirations for Apple icon Steve Jobs.

In 1983, when *Stranger Things* is set, Heathkit would have been in their prime, so the arrival of one of their radio kits would have been genuinely exciting to age-appropriate geeks. With one of these the boys would have been able to indulge in ham, or amateur radio, where members of the public could exchange messages and information with each other. These communities of amateur radio enthusiasts were like the Internet forums of their time and Mr. Clarke tells the boys that their new equipment would be powerful enough for them to contact people as far away as Australia. The Heath Company helped to fuel the burgeoning amateur radio scene across the world, as their cheap kits gave people access to equipment that they would previously have had to develop and construct from scratch. Easy to assemble and maintain, what these kits lacked in aesthetic quality they made up for in usability.

As well as perfectly evoking the period detail of the early 1980s, the radio also serves a part as a plot device in the show's first season. Needing a stronger radio in order for Eleven to contact Will, the boys sneak into the A.V. Club so she can use the Heathkit set. Eleven manages to connect with Will and play his voice over the set's speakers. The boys get to hear him say he was in a place that was 'dark and cold' before the set bursts into flames. Later, the school principal calls in a repairman to inspect the device, but unbeknownst to him it is a member of Hawkins Laboratory who is attempting to track down Eleven, who has clearly been alerted by the mysterious destruction of the equipment.

HEATON, CHARLIE

Born in Bridlington, England on 6 February 1992, Charlie Heaton is best known for his role as Jonathan Byers in *Stranger Things*. The actor moved to London to live with his dad when he was just sixteen, although his initial breakthrough in entertainment came via music, not acting. A talented musician, Heaton became the drummer for a band called Comanechi, a cult punk rock group that was perhaps best known for frontwoman Akiko Matsuura's fast and furious onstage style. Heaton joined the band for their world tour in 2013 travelling with bands like The Gossip.

After returning from the tour Heaton needed to earn some money so took his sister's advice and signed up at a commercial talent agency. 'My first job was a commercial for a Swiss insurance company,' he told *Interview Magazine*. 'It was an eight-minute short with a proper story arc, and it ended up getting a spot at Cannes Lions; I was lucky to avoid the commercials where you're their puppet.'

It wasn't long before Heaton was acting full time, starring in a smattering of short films before getting his onscreen break in the 2015 ITV crime drama *DCI Banks*. Later that year came a guest appearance in another ITV drama, *Vera* and two separate appearances on BBC One's long-running Saturday night staple, *Casualty*. Appearances on the silver screen soon followed with Heaton landing a leading role in the 2016 Sundance Festival darling *As You Are* before going on to star in Farren Blackburn's *Shut In* alongside the likes of Naomi Watts and child star Jacob Tremblay.

Meanwhile, in August 2015 Heaton was announced as one of the young stars of Netflix's new series *Stranger Things*. Speaking to *i-D* magazine Heaton reflected on his excitement after reading the script for the series. 'I'd never seen anything like it,' he admitted. 'The producers sent me a script as well as a trailer of all these different 80s movies cut together; it was the same trailer they used to sell the show to Netflix. I just remember thinking, "Wow, this is really different."'

Heaton has become the talk of Tinseltown following

Stranger Things' success, with many industry insiders marking his card as acting's next big thing, making comparisons with promising stars of the past like River Phoenix and Dane DeHaan. He's also become a staple of gossip columns thanks to his rumoured relationship with co-star Natalia Dyer, who plays Nancy Wheeler on the show.

HENDERSON, DUSTIN

The curly-haired, cap-wearing, chocolate pudding connoisseur Dustin Henderson is one of the central characters of *Stranger Things'* first season. Played by Gaten Matarazzo, Dustin is best friends with Mike, Will and Lucas.

As well as that curly hair, and penchant for trucker caps, what makes Dustin perhaps most recognizable is the absence of his two front teeth – which lead Hawkins Middle School's resident bullies to nickname him 'Toothless'. The reason behind Dustin's missing gnashers is a condition called cleidocranial dysplasia, a genetic disorder involving bone growth.

Like the other boys, Dustin is a keen member of the school A.V. Club and a regular competitor in the annual science fair. Indeed, Dustin is especially curious about science, as it is principally he who interacts with Mr. Clarke in order to better understand the theory behind things such as sensory deprivation and the Upside Down.

It is Dustin himself who explains the Upside Down

for the audience, comparing it to Dungeons & Dragons' Vale of Shadows. Later in the series he also shows off his smarts after he realises that none of the boys' compasses point true north, a side effect of the rift between two dimensions that has disrupted magnetic fields in Hawkins.

Like his friends, Dustin is also an unashamed geek. During the first episode he loses a bet with Will Byers for a copy of one of his X-Men comics. He is also a keen Dungeons & Dragons player; in the same episode, playing the role of the Dwarf in the boys' party, he initially advises Will to cast a protection spell when they come into contact with the Demogorgon during their game. He's always quick with a pop culture reference, whether it's comparing Eleven's powers to Professor X or suspecting the Chief of being Hawkins' own resident Lando Calrissian.

Despite his intelligence – both emotional and scientific – Dustin still delivers plenty of comic relief throughout the first season of *Stranger Things*. His love of snacks and his quick-witted responses to grown-ups, in particular Mr Clarke provide some of the best laugh-out-loud moments the show has to offer.

Throughout the show Dustin is the glue that holds the group together. He is also very in touch with his emotions for his age. We see this in the very first episode when he questions Nancy's odd behaviour and observes that she used to be cool. He is also the first to vocalise the conflict between Mike and Lucas when the two friends stop talking to each other after a bad fight, pointing out Lucas's jealousy over Mike's growing attachment to Eleven. His sensitive approach is even extended to Eleven who he welcomes to the group with open arms, quite literally, after she saves him and Mike from their school bullies during an incident at the quarry.

'I like how he's loyal to his friends and he's always there to keep trying to get people to get along, even if it doesn't work out all that well,' Gaten Matarazzo said of his character during an interview with the *Daily Beast* in August 2016. 'He's always trying his best to keep everyone in line.'

Indeed without Gaten's influence the character might have been very different. The Duffer Brothers have admitted in several interviews that Dustin was originally meant to be a more stereotypical character, but they re-wrote the part after casting the thirteen-year-old actor. 'I don't think we really understood who that character was,' Matt Duffer told the *Daily Beast*, 'and then we met Gaten and basically tailored the show to him.'

HOLLAND, BARBARA 'BARB'

Though she was a relatively minor character during *Stranger Things*' first season Barb has become one of the show's most endearing legacies, and a perennially popular talking point amongst the show's fans.

Played by Shannon Purser, Barbara Holland is a seventeen-year-old student at Hawkins High School and best friend of Nancy Wheeler. With her mop of curly hair and geeky glasses, Barb is presented as Nancy's sensible friend and it is no surprise then that she is initially cautious about her BFF's growing connection with bad boy Steve Harrington. Begrudgingly, however, she agrees to accompany Nancy to Steve's party, giving her a ride in her Volkswagen Cabrio.

At the party Barb cuts her hand while attempting to open a beer can with a knife, and then argues with Nancy who heads upstairs to bed with Steve. Sat alone by the swimming pool Barb's wound bleeds through her bandages, attracting the attention of the Monster from the Upside Down which drags her into the pool. Though her disappearance is covered up by the staff at Hawkins Laboratory, Barb's absence causes both Nancy and her parents to become concerned; it is not until Eleven enters the sensory deprivation tank that her fate is finally confirmed. It is Eleven who finds the grizzly sight of Barb's body strung up in the Hawkins Library and watches as a slug-like creature crawls from her mouth and across her face.

Purser herself tweeted that 'Barb wasn't supposed to be a big deal' and yet the Internet seemed to take no notice, with social media launching the bespectacled bit-part character to infamy. The hashtag #ImWithBarb became a trending topic on Twitter and Instagram with stars like American actor John Stamos sharing their love of the doe-eyed character. Following that, the hashtag #WeAreAllBarb gained popularity among social media users as they shared their own geeky high school photographs in honour of the missing character.

But the love for Barb didn't stop there. In August 2016, Barb was described as a 'Style Icon' by Jo Ellison in the *Financial Times*: 'Barb is the perfect expression of geek chic: a strawberry-blonde valedictorian who wears red-rimmed spectacles and mom jeans, she bears an uncanny resemblance to Scooby-Doo's Velma, and accessorises her look with a bubble-gum pink ring-folder and floral bound diary. With her caramel-coloured sweaters and winceyette pie-crust collar blouses she could easily be an extra from the latest Gucci campaign (if Gucci cast girls who look "normal"-sized).'

Elsewhere media outlets were quick to pen all manner of essays in honour of the prematurely departed Barb. From *Vanity Fair* to Vulture, acres of column inches were dedicated to the character's reactions, her most quotable lines, and even her reaction shots. Vulture's Brian Moylan took things one step further by exploring what had made Barb so popular, especially in comparison to Nancy. 'Nancy is an archetype created through an evil conspiracy launched by Wes Craven, John Hughes, and Molly Ringwald sometime during the Reagan administration. It's a conspiracy more dangerous than nuclear proliferation, because everyone is still trying to be Nancy and hating who they really are: Barb.'

Fans as well as critics continued to share their love of Barb. 'Wanted' posters of the character started to crop up on the web, and she even got her own Reddit thread.

YouTube star Dr Chorizo even released a loving rap tribute to Barb entitled 'R.I.P. Barb – A Stranger Things Tribute' that garnered more than a quarter of a million views online. In LA someone created a Barb graffiti mural with the words 'In loving memory of Barb' emblazoned above a drawing of her face.

Speaking to the HitFix website about the Internet's reaction to the character Matt Duffer said: 'I'm surprised and also not surprised at the outpouring of love for Barb, because that was something everyone felt on set. The fact that people aren't really following up on her disappearance to the same degree they are with Will makes her that much more of a tragic character.'

The show's creators also promised that Barb's fate wouldn't be forgotten in the second season of *Stranger Things*. 'We'll make sure there's some justice for Barb,' Matt Duffer told IGN. 'People get very frustrated, understandably, that the town doesn't seem to be really dealing with Barb. That stuff is all happening. We're just not spending any screen time on it. It's not like her parents are like "Oh Barb left. She died!" Season 1 actually takes place over the course of six or seven days – it's a really short period of time. So part of what we want to do with hypothetical Season 2 is to explore the repercussions of everything that happened.'

Barb's online fame became so powerful that the character was even featured as part of host Jimmy Fallon's intro to the 2017 Golden Globe Awards. Appearing as part of a musical number that aped movie musical *La*

La Land, the cast of *Stranger Things* performed a rap that confirmed that Barb was still alive: the camera cut to a shot of Barb being resurrected from Steve Harrington's pool complete with a backing troupe of Barb lookalikes. The reaction to the skit on social media was so pronounced that Millie Bobby Brown had to confirm in a later interview that the character was indeed dead, for fear of disappointing dedicated Barb fans when season two rolls around.

'HOLLY, JOLLY'

'Holly, Jolly' is the name of the third episode from season one of *Stranger Things*. The episode was directed by the show's executive producer Shawn Levy and written by Jessica Mecklenburg.

The only episode of the first season with a title that doesn't begin with the word 'the', it is also the first episode to feature action that takes place within the Upside Down. That action revolves around Barb's death with the glasses-wearing fan-favourite thrashing around in what looks to be an alternate version of Steve's pool. She yells for help but is eventually dragged down into the depths by the Demogorgon.

The episode gives us some more insight into the life of Eleven. Flashbacks show us the time she spent incarcerated in the subterranean depths of Hawkins Laboratory. Her powers are demonstrated as she crushes a Coke can with her mind, but her despicable treatment is also shown when Dr Brenner attempts to make her kill a cat, only to toss her into solitary confinement when she refuses to participate. The ensuing struggle sees Eleven kill two of Brenner's employees.

Back in the present day of 1983 we also get to learn more about the sinister laboratory through Chief Hopper's investigations, as well as his research into Project MKUltra. Elsewhere Joyce continues to communicate with her son, in what are some of Winona Ryder's most powerful scenes from the whole first season, and the episode ends with the apparent discovery of Will's body in the Hawkins quarry.

HOPPER, DIANE

Formerly married to Chief Jim Hopper for seven years, Diane (played by Jerri Tubbs) divorced her husband following the death of their daughter, Sarah. During the first season we see Diane through flashbacks, playing with her family at the park and later watching on as doctors attempt to resuscitate her daughter. Though she doesn't actually appear in the Hawkins universe of 1983, she does speak with Chief Hopper on the telephone, where her concern for her former spouse is evident, despite the fact she has married a man called Bill and had a second child with him.

HOPPER, JIM

Played by David Harbour, Jim Hopper is the Hawkins Chief of Police and the resident antihero of *Stranger Things*. Born sometime in the 1940s Hopper is an overweight alcoholic with a penchant for pills and a habit for scathing sarcasm. His pronounced transformation in the first season rivals that of Eleven's: over the space of eight episodes, he transforms from misanthropic sceptic to badass hero.

Hopper wasn't always quite as curmudgeonly as the series initially portrays him. Though he is originally from Hawkins, and attended school with Joyce Byers whom it is implied he dated, Hopper moved away to the city with his wife Diane. There they had a daughter, Sarah, and Hopper worked in the police force. However his idyllic life was shattered when his daughter died of cancer, a tragedy that also affected his marriage to Diane, which ended in divorce.

Hopper moved back to Hawkins in 1979 and became Chief of Police, but still bears the scars of his daughter's death, and abuses alcohol and prescription medication. He drinks on the job and smokes like a chimney. He is also shown to have a habit for one-night stands, rather than forming long-term relationships. He hates children, he's sarcastic to everyone... In fact you start the season wondering if he's the bad guy, only to find yourself first pumping the air by the end of season one when he saves Will and leaves a box of Eggos out in the woods for Eleven.

Initially, though, Hopper's approach to Will Byers' disappearance is sceptical. He first suggests to Joyce that Will is simply 'playing hookie' and later, when Joyce claims that Will has contacted her, he dismisses her claims as grief-fuelled illusions. But it is Hopper's investigations that ultimately lead to the rescue of Will Byers and the uncovering of Hawkins Laboratory's nefarious dealings. He starts to suspect the government institution after following a lead and realizing the laboratory had faked their security videos to cover something up.

It is also Hopper who discovers evidence of Dr Brenner's involvement with Project MKUltra after searching through newspaper clippings at the library. Not even the discovery of Will Byers' body could stop his investigation. Initially believing his search has come to a tragic conclusion, Hopper works off of a hunch, and Joyce's insistence that the body in the morgue is not her son, and tracks down the truth. We see that he isn't afraid to bend the rules in search of the truth, first using his fists to extract information from the State Trooper who apparently discovered the body in the quarry for information, and later breaking into the morgue to examine the body for himself.

After realising that Byers' body is a fake, Hopper breaks into the Laboratory and discovers a cell with a child's bed in it and the Gate to the Upside Down, but before he is able to investigate he is knocked unconscious by the Laboratory staff and wakes up back in his home, which he discovers has been bugged. It won't be the last time Hopper breaks into the laboratory, though. After helping to rescue the boys and Eleven, he and Joyce return to pass through the Gate and rescue Will from the Upside Down, but not before striking a deal with Dr Brenner to trade Eleven's whereabouts for the boys' safety.

Despite finding Will in the Upside Down and administering CPR to bring him back to life, Hopper's actions mean that he is regarded as a villain at the end of the first season, a point that is emphasised when he is shown getting into a car with what we presume are agents from Hawkins Laboratory. However there are also still signs of redemption for the police chief: he has swiped some food (including Eleven's beloved Eggos waffles) from a Christmas party and leaves it in a concealed box in the woods. It all sums up Hopper's character – a conflicted hero who will go to just about any lengths to find the truth.

It's no wonder then that fans and critics alike have pointed to Hopper as perhaps *Stranger Things*' most intriguing character. Harbour himself summed up Hopper's appeal nicely: 'It's such a sophisticated, three-dimensional character and what the character goes through is so amazing,' Harbour said in an interview with CNN in 2016. 'He has all these issues and all this pain that he masks with sarcasm and with this acting out and this shtick that he's developed. Then you start to unravel that throughout the series, and you start to see that this is just a broken man who's trying to survive. That type of complexity opens up empathy for all sorts of people. That's wonderful and rare to be able to play a character that rich.'

The Duffer Brothers agreed. 'David loved Hopper because he felt that the role harkened back to an old-school type of Hollywood hero,' they told *Entertainment Weekly*. 'Hopper's not a superhero. He's screwed up, he screws up, he's not afraid to make an ass of himself, and he solves problems with both his brains and his fists.'

HOPPER, SARAH

Daughter of Diane and Jim Hopper, Sarah died of cancer at a young age. Played by Elle Graham, we only see Sarah through flashbacks – once when she has a panic attack while playing in the park, and again when she is receiving chemotherapy in the hospital after her cancer diagnosis. It is Sarah's death that drives Jim and Diane apart, and probably drives Hopper to alcoholism.

I

INSPIRATION BOARD

Noah Schapp, who plays Will Byers on the show, revealed that the Duffer Brothers used an 'Inspiration Board' to help guide the show's creation. In an interview with *Entertainment Tonight* the young actor said: 'I remember [Matt and Ross Duffer] had this big board when I was in one of the later callbacks and it said "inspiration board", and it had a bunch of movie posters with movie names on it.'

Those movie posters included the likes of *Poltergeist*, *E.T.*, *The Goonies* and *Stand by Me*. The Duffer Brothers cite all of them as inspirations when they were growing up and so it is no surprise to see nods to them throughout the series.

Of course those titles would have meant nothing to *Stranger Things*' childhood stars who are far too young to have watched them. So the Duffers ensured that the child actors watched the shows ahead of shooting in order to share their cinematic influences and set the tone for the series as a whole.

INSTAGRAM

The performances of the *Stranger Things* cast have been so convincing that it's sometimes hard to believe these are actors, especially actors who, in many cases, haven't even gone through puberty at the time of production. But thanks to their Instagram accounts we've got to know the actors away from the spooky goings-on in Hawkins and found out they are every bit as amazing. The young cast members are particularly active on social media, interacting with fans, taking selfies, and generally doing whatever any average teenager would do with their spare time.

The key accounts to follow if you want to keep up to date with the cast are:

Millie Bobby Brown (Eleven) – instagram.com/
    milliebobbybrown
Gaten Matarazzo (Dustin Henderson) – instagram.com/
    gatenm123
Noah Schnapp (Will Byers) – instagram.com/
    noahschnapp

Finn Wolfhard (Mike Wheeler) – instagram.com/
finnwolfhardofficial

Caleb McLaughlin (Lucas Sinclair) – instagram.com/
therealcalebmclaughlin

Charlie Heaton (Jonathan Byers) – instagram.com/
charlie.r.heaton

Joe Keery (Steve Harrington) – instagram.com/uncle_
jezzy

Natalia Dyer (Nancy Wheeler) – instagram.com/
nattyiceofficial

Shannon Purser (Barbara Holland) – instagram.com/
uncle_jezzy

IT

With their obvious passions for all things Stephen King it should come as little surprise that the Duffer Brothers tried to pitch a modern-day remake of *It*, King's infamous 1986 crown creeper. A 1,000-page epic that takes place across two different timezones, *It* tells the story of four childhood friends taking on an evil clown called Pennywise. The novel is, at the time of writing, currently being adapted for the big screen by Cary Fukunaga, but in different circumstances, it could have been the Duffer Brothers behind the adaptation; the duo have confirmed that they pitched their ideas to Warner Bros. before starting work on *Stranger Things*, only to be turned down by the studio at the time.

IVES, BECKY

Portrayed by Amy Seimetz, Becky Ives is a character in the first season of *Stranger Things*. First seen in episode six, Becky is a caregiver for her sister Terry who was part of Dr Brenner's Project MKUltra experiments. It is Becky who confirms the existence of the government experiments that Hopper has read about in newspaper clippings. She also confirms that Terry believed her daughter to be alive, despite her supposed miscarriage and the absence of a birth certificate.

IVES, JANE

Jane is the daughter that Terry Ives supposedly gave birth to while undergoing experiments at the hands of Dr Brenner and the MKUltra project. Though Becky Ives suggests that Jane was miscarried during the third trimester, Terry believes her daughter is alive and that she was taken from her due to her 'abilities'. Though it is never overtly stated the audience is led to believe by the conclusion of the first season that Jane Ives is in fact Eleven's real name.

IVES, TERRY

Played by Aimee Mullins, Terry Ives is Eleven's real mother – though the existence of her child was covered up by Dr Brenner and his team. Terry took part in the

Project MKUltra experiments during college in the hope of 'expanding the boundaries of the mind'. As part of the experiments she was subjected to psychedelic drugs while undergoing sensory deprivation.

After discovering that Will's body was fake, Hopper teams up with Joyce to visit Terry, but upon their arrival Becky informs them that they are 'about five years too late', no doubt referring to her sister's catatonic state. The meeting is the last we see of Terry, although in amongst the newspaper clippings about Will that we see on Hopper's wall, there is one headline that mentions Ives' disgust at the Hawkins Laboratory, though it is not confirmed whether it is Terry or Becky who has been talking to reporters.

J

JAMES

Played by Cade Jones, James is a bully at Hawkins Middle School who, alongside Troy, regularly torments Mike and his friends.

JAWS (1975)

Though the Duffer Brothers are undoubtedly influenced by Steven Spielberg's work in the 1980s, the film that helped the director to make his name is not overlooked during *Stranger Things*. *Jaws* established Spielberg beyond doubt as one of Hollywood's hottest talents. Like *Stranger Things* it revolves around a small town that is being haunted by a monster, and like *Stranger Things* that monster is attracted by the smell of blood. In the Duffers' series, when Barb is attacked, and blood from her wound drops into the swimming pool water, it could have been plucked directly from Spielberg's movie. As if to hammer the point home the Duffers also provide a visual reference to cinema's most famous shark, as in episode seven, Jonathan's bedroom is shown to have a *Jaws* poster adorning its walls.

JEN

Jen is Mr Clarke's partner. She is shown cuddling up to the moustachioed science teacher watching *The Thing* when Dustin calls his tutor for advice on how to build a sensory deprivation tank. She is played by Jackie Dallas.

JONATHAN'S MIXTAPE

'I made you a new mixtape. There's some stuff on there I think you really might like,' Jonathan Byers tells his brother Will during the first season of *Stranger Things*. The Byers boys would share two mixtapes in the series, symbolising a bond between the brothers.

The first mixtape is shown during a flashback to 1982. Looking at the handwritten notes on the cassette cover we can see it contains songs like 'Should I Stay or Should I Go' by The Clash and 'Atmosphere' by Joy Division. There are also unnamed tracks from Television, David Bowie and The Smiths (which is actually one of the rare historical inaccuracies within the show, given that the band wouldn't have made it to America until a few years after the action is set) . During the first season's finale Jonathan gifts his brother a second mixtape in the hospital, a sign that the two have been reconciled.

Jonathan's mixtape took on a life of its own outside of the series, where fans created playlists dedicated to the elder Byers boy's song selections. Eventually British hip-hop artist DJ Yoda released his own *Stranger Things* mixtape online, which weaves together quotes from the show with eighties classics ranging from New Order to Tangerine Dream.

K

KEERY, JOE

Joe Keery is an actor and musician who is best known for playing bouffant bad boy Steve Harrington. Born in Massachusetts on 24 April 1992, Keery was the second of five children, and was persuaded into acting by his eldest sister, while he was attending Newburyport High School. Upon finishing high school in 2010, Keery enrolled on a theatre course at Chicago's DePaul University where he appeared in several stage shows, musicals and productions.

After graduating, Keery got his first big break in a KFC commercial before landing bit parts in US dramas *Empire* and *Chicago Fire*. He also made his silver screen debut in 2015 in Stephen Cone's indie film *Henry*

Gamble's Birthday Party. Keery claims to have attended more than a hundred auditions since finishing school, and fortunately, one of those was for the Duffer Brothers' *Stranger Things*. He initially auditioned for the role of Jonathan, but was called back to read for the part of Steve. The role was his first true break into the business – in fact Keery was actually working at a burger joint when he found out he'd landed the role.

Outside of his screen work and indeed outside his work in burger joints, Keery also has a passion for music: he is a singer, songwriter and guitarist, and a member of a psych rock band called Post Animal, a big part of the Chicago music scene and who have been likened to such bands as Tame Impala and The Shins.

KING, STEPHEN

Though there is an avalanche of cinematic references strewn throughout *Stranger Things*' first season, the show's DNA is also spliced with its fair share of literary nods in the direction of Stephen King.

King, as if he needs any introduction, is an author who has penned 54 novels and more than 200 short stories featuring everyone from killer clowns to telekinetic teens. His novels have sold more than 350 million copies worldwide and many have made it to our screens in the form of television shows and movies. King sold his first short story in 1967 aged just twenty, and in 1973 his first novel was published. That novel was *Carrie*, just one of a laundry list of iconic titles that includes *The Shining*, *The Dead Zone*, *Firestarter* and *The Dark Tower* series.

Apart from perhaps Steven Spielberg, it's probably fair to say that Stephen King is the biggest single influence on *Stranger Things* in its first season. Indeed Matt and Ross Duffer themselves have repeatedly spoken about drawing inspiration from King's work. Speaking to the *Wall Street Journal* in 2016 Matt Duffer explained the brothers' love of King's catalogue:

'The books of Stephen King were a big inspiration. It was those films and books that were such a big part of our childhoods. What made all these stories so great, and connected all of them, was that they explored that point where the ordinary meets the extraordinary. That's what we wanted the show to do because, when we were growing up, we were just regular kids living in the suburbs of North Carolina playing Dungeons & Dragons with our friends, so when we watched these films or read these books, we felt [like those characters].'

Even during the pitching process King's influence was never far from the Duffer Brothers' minds. When presenting their ideas to networks, they produced a twenty-page pitching book with eighties-era visuals that they stuffed inside the cover of an old copy of Stephen King's *Firestarter*.

It's no surprise then that there's a multitude of King references scattered throughout the finished script. For example in the first episode when Joyce flashes back to her conversation with her son Will in Castle Byers, and he tells her he doesn't get scared anymore she replies: 'Oh yeah? Not even of... clowns?'

Then there are the characters themselves. The group of boys certainly evoke the heroes of King novels such as *The Dreamcatcher*, while their adventure along the railroad tracks in search of the Gate from episode five is an apparent reference to the movie *Stand By Me*, which was based on the Stephen King short story 'The Body'. That title is also evoked in the name of *Stranger Things'* fourth episode.

Finally there's Eleven, whose character is no doubt inspired by two of the author's more infamous heroines: Carrie and *Firestarter*'s Charlie McGee. The series emphasizes these influences in a tongue-in-cheek fashion. When Terry Ives, believed to be Eleven's biological mother, is visited by Joyce and Hopper and asked if she feels that her daughter was born with special abilities, Terry's sister Becky responds: 'Read any Stephen King?'

L

LEVY, SHAWN

Born in Montreal, Canada in 1968, Shawn Levy is an actor, director and producer who served as Executive Producer on the first season of *Stranger Things*. Levy first found a middling career as an actor with his appearances limited to low budget horror flicks like *Zombie Nightmare* (1986) and guest spots in shows like *21 Jump Street* and *Beverly Hills 90210*. But it is behind the camera where Levy has come to leave his mark on the entertainment industry.

On the small screen Levy has directed episodes of series including *The Secret World of Alex Mack*, *Lassie*, and Netflix's *The Unbreakable Kimmy Schmidt*. He's also directed for the big screen, helming Hollywood flicks including *Just Married*, the *Night at the Museum* series, and *Real Steel*. More recently his name has been attached to a screen adaptation of the popular *Uncharted* video game franchise.

Through his production company 21 Laps Entertainment, Levy has also been responsible for helping to bring some iconic entertainment to our screens. For cinema, Levy has helped produce *Date Night* and *Arrival* while notable successes on the small screen have included ABC's sitcom *Last Man Standing*, starring Tim Allen, and of course Netflix's *Stranger Things*.

Levy describes *Stranger Things* as a 'diamond in the rough'. He met with the Duffer Brothers when they were in the process of pitching the series and decided immediately to help them shepherd their story to our screens. Like the brothers, he is a self-confessed Spielberg fan, and even got to work with his idol on his movie *Real Steel*. Not only did Levy produce *Stranger Things*' first season, he also directed its third and fourth episodes.

Speaking to *Variety* in 2016 Levy said of his directorial duties: 'It was clear to me I needed to buy the Duffers time to write the rest of the season and I didn't trust an outsider to come and direct any shows in season one. A big part of it was I did it for the team and did it for the Brothers. The selfish agenda was by that point I had fallen so hard in love with the show and I knew episode three and four had some of the juiciest scenes and visuals of the season... I've made 11 movies and I have rarely been as inspired as I felt directing these episodes.'

He's not lying either. Episodes three and four – 'Chapter Three: Holly, Jolly' and 'Chapter Four: The Body' – feature such iconic scenes as Eleven's sensory deprivation, Joyce's communication with Will through the Christmas lights, and Hopper's investigation into the body found in the quarry. At the time of writing, Levy has also confirmed that he will return to direct two episodes in the show's second season.

Not content with his work behind the camera Levy also got to feature in front of it: he has a brief cameo as a coroner in episode four. Nevertheless, he has admitted he cut most of his scenes from the episode as he does not like watching himself as an actor.

LIGHTS

Lights play an important role in *Stranger Things*' first season, representing one of the few means through which people can communicate between the Upside Down and real life Hawkins. Early on in the show lights are used as an early indicator of paranormal activity: a lightbulb in Will's shed flickers and smashes before he is taken by the Demogorgon, and continues to act as a precursor for the Monster's arrival throughout the rest of the season.

Joyce is the first person to realise that Will is communicating to her through the light. In response she rigs up in her home an elaborate system of fairy lights – bought with an advance from her job at Melvald's General Store. Creating a rudimentary Ouija board of sorts, she paints letters on the wall with corresponding lights. This provides her with a means through which she can establish basic communication with her son in the Upside Down.

In the final episode the importance of lights is once again stressed as Joyce and Hopper look for Will in the Byers house. As they walk through the hallways the lights that are strung up across the ceilings of the property start to light up, tracking their movement – suggesting that the lights provide some kind of connection between the two dimensions. Likewise it's also no coincidence that Dr Brenner and the bad men disguise themselves as employees of Hawkins Power & Light when they are in the field.

M

M. NIGHT SHYAMALAN

The director who is famed for his twist endings and early films including *The Sixth Sense* and *Unbreakable* has been something of a mentor to the Duffer Brothers, taking them under his wing and adding them to the writers room on *Wayward Pines*, the TV show he executive produces. During an interview with entertainment website Digital Spy, Shyamalan even joked that he'd like them to return the favour for an episode of their show's second season. 'My boys who do *Stranger Things*, they did *Wayward Pines* for me,' he said. 'They were 'round my house and I was like, "Well, you can hire me back, guys!"'

MAKEOVER

In the fourth episode of *Stranger Things'* first season, Mike, Dustin and Lucas give Eleven a makeover so that she might fit in at Hawkins Middle School. Using make-up, a wig and pink dress they attempt to transform the shaven-headed teen. Mike describes the end result as 'pretty', something that Eleven herself echoes when she looks in the mirror.

The scene is another reference to 1980s entertainment, this time a nod towards Steven Spielberg's *E.T.*: Eleven's disguise echoes that given to the titular alien by Gertie in the 1982 movie. It also pays homage to the makeover montage that became a common stereotype of movies of the era, with Ally Sheedy's transformation in *The Breakfast Club* a prime example.

Eleven's makeover moment wasn't without its controversies however, with some critics citing that scene as an example of sexism in the show. In *The Atlantic*, Lenika Cruz wrote: 'Eleven is clearly the token girl of the group – recalling the "Smurfette Principle" trope that pervaded children's TV during [the 1980s] – but the show doesn't display much self-awareness on this point. There's even a textbook "makeover scene" involving a wig, some makeup, and a dress that leads the boys to behold a transformed Eleven in awe.'

Similar sentiments were expressed by Shannon Keating on BuzzFeed: 'Eleven is at home in a long history of young female characters whose ultimate worth is dictated by her romantic appeal to boys – someone who must first become desirably feminine before she can fully claim that worthiness at all. That premise is all the more galling in a show where Eleven is a) the hero, and b) prepubescent. Why on earth does she need to be worrying about attracting boys when she's a literal child – one preoccupied with saving people in mortal danger, no less?

'Even though Eleven didn't make the choice to shave her head, *Stranger Things* presumes that the ultra-feminine is girlhood's default, a natural and obvious preference. To be masculine-presenting, pop culture tells us, is to be weird, abnormal, ugly, bad (in another word: queer). Prescribed femininity is therefore a cure-all: If a girl can be pretty, she can be available to men. And in 2016, as in the '80s, a girl is still supposed to be both.'

MARISSA

Marissa (Christi Waldon) is an employee at the Hawkins Public Library who helps Chief Hopper and Officer Powell to track down information on Dr Brenner and Project MKUltra from the archives. She is not overly friendly to Hopper, however, and it is revealed that she and the police chief were once lovers, although it seems like their relationship ended on bad terms with Marissa claiming the police chief 'wasted' her time.

MATARAZZO, GATEN

Born on 8 September 2002, Gaten Matarazzo plays the character of Dustin Henderson, a favourite of many *Stranger Things*' fans. *Stranger Things* was Matarazzo's first recurring role on a TV show, but his earliest TV appearance came with a second season episode of hit US show, *The Blacklist* that aired in February 2015.

Originally from New Jersey, Matarazzo's career started out on stage, initially in a Broadway production of *Priscilla, Queen of the Desert* at the Palace Theatre in 2011. He then returned to Broadway in 2014 to play Gavroche in the Imperial Theatre's production of *Les Misérables*.

Matarazzo is instantly recognizable thanks to his mop of curly hair and his missing front teeth, the latter caused by a condition called cleidocranial dysplasia that affects bone growth. Though he now wears fake teeth, Matarazzo has claimed in interviews that his condition has previously affected his chances of getting onscreen roles and that he has in fact been previously turned down on account of his lisp and size. Using his newfound fame from the show Matarazzo has been working to raise awareness of his condition, helping to fundraise for a cleidocranial dysplasia charity called CCD Smiles, by releasing his own limited edition *Ghostbusters*-inspired t-shirt.

Matarazzo's disability did nothing to deter the Duffer Brothers from casting him in *Stranger Things*. In fact, they embraced the actor with open arms. 'Gaten was everything,' Matt Duffer said in an interview with Uproxx in July 2016. 'What's so cool about television, we had cast all the kids, and we only had one script written at that point. I think Dustin was a much more clichéd character. He was just the nerd. He didn't have that much interesting personality. We talked a lot: we don't quite understand him as a character. The minute we saw Gaten's tape, we knew he would be in the show as Dustin. The disease we say he has in the show, he has in real life: he has no collarbone and no front teeth. He's very much the person that you see in the show.'

Matt Duffer also pointed out that Gaten took an online quiz to find out which character he'd be on the show, and ended up getting Dustin. 'We basically wrote it for Gaten, and so much of the credit for the character goes entirely to Gaten,' he said in the same interview. 'All the love that he's getting, he deserves. He's an amazing kid. He's very very funny. The hardest thing about shooting with the kids is that Gaten made them laugh so much, sometimes it was hard to get the scene down without someone breaking out with laughter. He's just a funny funny kid. His comic timing is impeccable. I think he's so special.'

MCLAUGHLIN, CALEB

Born 13 October 2001, Caleb McLaughlin plays Lucas Sinclair in *Stranger Things*. Originally from Carmel, a small town in suburban New York, Caleb has studied dance and singing at both the Happy Feet dance school and the Harlem School of the Arts. It comes as no surprise to discover, then, that like some of his co-stars Caleb has appeared on the Broadway stage; he made his breakthrough playing the role of Young Simba in the Minskoff Theatre's production of the *Lion King* from 2012–14. It was during his time on Broadway that Caleb befriended fellow *Stranger Things* co-star Gaten Matarazzo who was in *Les Misérables* at the time. The two young actors met in a nearby park that child stars use to chill out.

But Caleb's acting credentials don't just involve Broadway musicals. Before *Stranger Things* he had built up quite the TV resume, including appearances in US staples such as *Law & Order: Special Victims Unit*, *Unforgettable*, *Forever*, and *Shades of Blue*. *Stranger Things* was his first recurring role, though, and he beat out hundreds of other kids for the chance to play Lucas. His path to his part wasn't an easy one, however. It all started when he sent the casting director a tape of himself that he and his mum had put together. Then he underwent a series of Skype auditions and chats with the production crew before finally flying out to LA to meet the rest of the *Stranger Things* cast.

Caleb spent a lot of time on the publicity circuit with his fellow stars following *Stranger Things'* release, but he still returned to the small screen in 2017 for his critically acclaimed turn in *The New Edition Story*. It was a three-part mini-series about the rise of 1980s R&B sensations New Edition in the early 1980s, and he won plaudits for his portrayal of a young Ricky Bell. He even got the thumbs-up from Bell himself who had worked closely with the young actor on set.

MELVALD'S GENERAL STORE

Located in Downtown Hawkins, Melvald's General Store is named after its owner Donald Melvald, played by Charles Lawlor, who is Joyce Byers' boss. Melvald's Store stocks just about everything from Christmas lights to phones. The day after Will's disappearance Donald agrees to advance Joyce two weeks salary in order for her to buy a new phone. Later he serves her when she returns to buy another phone alongside the store's supply of Christmas lights.

MINORITY REPORT (2002)

Yet another Steven Spielberg movie to be referenced in *Stranger Things* is one of his more recent classics: his futuristic crime thriller *Minority Report*. The reference specifically occurs in the scene where Eleven enters her makeshift sensory deprivation tank in the Hawkins Middle School gymnasium. The top down shot recalls the way in which Spielberg filmed the precognitive triplets in his blockbuster.

MIRKWOOD

The Mirkwood is the name given to the road and surrounding forest that leads up to Hawkins National Laboratory. Located where the roads of Cornwallis and Kerley meet it is on this road that Will Byers first encounters the Monster. It is also where Mike and his friends first meet Eleven, while out searching for their friend themselves.

Mirkwood is also a reference to a dark forest that is found in J. R. R. Tolkien's *The Hobbit* as well as *The Lord of the Rings*. The Mirkwood is said to be where the character of Legolas originated from.

MKULTRA

Project MKUltra is the name of the CIA-sanctioned project that created Eleven in *Stranger Things*. Chief Hopper found out about the project through newspaper clippings where he uncovered Dr Brenner's involvement in the experiments and Terry Ives' accusations that those resulted in her daughter being kidnapped at birth. Some of the details of the experiments are revealed when Hopper and Joyce Byers visit Terry and her sister Becky to find out more about their story.

During their visit we are told that Terry participated in the experiments during college, and that part of the project entailed her being subjected to psychedelic drugs including LSD, as well as sensory deprivation environments. Unbeknownst to Terry she was pregnant at the time of the experiment, and the audience is left to conclude that the conditions of the experiment helped to give Eleven her powers.

It may seem far-fetched but *Stranger Things'* explanation of Project MKUltra actually skirts pretty close to the real life experiments that were carried out by the CIA during the Cold War. Beginning in the early 1950s and continuing until 1973, Project MKUltra was the codename given to a series of mind control projects intended to develop techniques to force confessions through interrogations and torture.

Conducted at more than eighty institutions, the clandestine operation was wide-ranging and explored all manner of techniques to manipulate people's mental states including hallucinogenic drugs, hypnosis, sensory deprivation, isolation, and various forms of psychological torture. Millions of dollars were poured into the project as Cold War paranoia and reports of similar mind control techniques being used in China, Russia and North Korea made it to the USA. Though the initial aim of the project was to develop a means to force confessions out of Soviet spies, the project extended to an investigation into developing drugs that could be used to control foreign leaders – most notably Fidel Castro.

The project first came to public attention in 1975 after President Gerald Ford ordered a Congressional Investigation into the activity of the CIA on American citizens. Further detail was revealed in 1977 after a Freedom of Information request revealed a cache of 20,000 documents relating to Project MKUltra. Despite light being shed on some aspects of the project, most evidence relating to it had been destroyed by the CIA in 1973 which has only helped to fuel the sense of intrigue surrounding the experiments that were being conducted. The project was also particularly controversial as it was revealed that many of the experiments were conducted on US citizens without their knowledge.

Stranger Things isn't the first piece of pop culture to explore the CIA's secret MKUltra research. The experimentations also influenced sci-fi shows such as *The X Files* and *Fringe* as well as playing an important role in movies such as *The Manchurian Candidate*, and George Clooney's comedy *The Men Who Stare at Goats*.

MODINE, MATTHEW

Born on 22 March 1959, Matthew Modine plays Dr Brenner in *Stranger Things*. A veteran of both small and silver screen, Modine is perhaps most famous for his role as Private Joker in Stanley Kubrick's iconic Vietnam war flick *Full Metal Jacket* (1987) as well as a recurring part as Sullivan Groff on *Weeds*.

Modine did not audition for his role in *Stranger Things*. Instead his involvement came about after the Duffer Brothers approached him directly. Fans of his previous work, they wrote him a letter laying out their plans for the show and the world they would create. That was enough to get Modine on the phone, and their passion convinced him to sign on to play the head of Hawkins Laboratory – and one of the chief antagonists of the show's first season.

After joining the cast Modine had very specific ideas for how he wanted Dr Brenner to look, speak and act. He told observer.com: 'I had very specific ideas about Brenner's behavior. How Brenner's hair would look – I wanted Brenner's appearance to recall Robert Shaw's character in *Battle of the Bulge* – and my clothes be clean and meticulous like Cary Grant's suit in *North by Northwest*. The Duffers had written the character as an unshaved man in jeans and plaid shirts. And I also wanted to say less, or rather, to only speak when Brenner had something important to say or ask. The Duffers happily united behind these suggestions and merged them into their vision.'

'THE MONSTER'

'The Monster' is the name of the sixth episode of *Stranger Things*' first season. Written by Jessie Nickson-Lopez and directed by the Duffer Brothers the episode offers something of a back story for the season's principal antagonist, the Demogorgon.

It begins with Nancy escaping from the Upside Down, but not before she spies the Monster eating the deer carcass that it dragged there with him. It is not, though, the only time we see the Demogorgon during this episode – during a flashback later on, we see Eleven making contact with the Monster at the behest of Dr Brenner.

The rest of the episode also fills in the blanks of the Monster's origins. Lucas discovers that the magnetic north of his compass points to Hawkins Laboratory, confirming to the boys that the Demogorgon originated from inside the facility. Elsewhere Joyce and Hopper visit Terry Ives, and their exchange with the catatonic woman is an origin story of sorts, except this time it deals with Eleven and not the monster from the Upside Down.

The episode also features Jonathan's fight with Steve after the latter defaced the cinema sign, as well as Mike and Dustin's showdown with Troy, which is eventually ended after the intervention of Eleven.

MONSTERS INC.

For a series packed with child stars there's plenty for the actors on *Stranger Things* to be scared about. Conscious of the impact that the show's Monster had on the toddlers that were on set, the Duffer Brothers decided to tell the young actors that the Monster was just like the characters they would find in *Monsters Inc.* After that they treated the on-set rendering of the faceless beast as their friend.

'MONTAUK'

'Montauk' was the original name that the Duffer Brothers had given to their series before eventually changing the show's title to *Stranger Things*. The name came from a small seaside town on Long Island that was supposed to be the setting for the show, before production had to be moved to Atlanta for cost purposes.

The choice of the town of Montauk was not random either. The town is at the centre of a long-running conspiracy theory about the Montauk Project, a series of experiments that were supposedly carried out by the US Army at Camp Hero after World War II. The experiments are said to have involved psychological warfare, psychic abilities and even the accidental opening of portals to other dimensions. If that sounds familiar to *Stranger Things'* first season it's because it is. In fact the original script for *Stranger Things'* opening episode was based closely on the Montauk conspiracy theories.

Stranger Things isn't the first script to use Montauk as its setting either. The TV series *The Affair* was set there, and the town is even referenced by the character of Quint in Steven Spielberg's *Jaws* who boasts that he 'caught a 16-footer off of Montauk'.

THE MONTAUK PROJECT: EXPERIMENTS IN TIME

The Montauk Project: Experiments in Time is the first in a series of five science-fiction novels written by Preston B. Nichols and Peter Moon, and first published in 1992. The books were written in the first person and included original photographs and drawings of equipment supposedly used by the government. This style, alongside its links with the Montauk project conspiracy theories, has led many people to believe that they are indeed first-hand accounts of government experimentation. The novels include several details that will be familiar to *Stranger Things* fans including a secret subterranean government base, alternate dimensions, monsters, and children with psychic abilities.

MOUTH-BREATHER

Mouth-breather is one piece of modern American vocabulary that Mike teaches the language-deprived Eleven during the first season of *Stranger Things*. The insult is just one of the terms that the boys have for their Middle School bullies:

'I was tripped by this mouth-breather Troy, OK?" Mike tells Eleven in episode three.

'Mouth-breather?' she asks.

'Yeah, you know… a dumb person, a knucklehead… I don't know why I just didn't tell you. Everyone at school knows. I just, didn't want you to think I was such a wastoid, you know?'

The insult bonds Mike and Eleven together and is hurled in the direction of everyone from high school bullies to controlling adults over the course of the series. It's also entirely period-appropriate. Though the term was first used in medical circles in the early 20th century to describe children with respiratory conditions, from the 1960s the term entered the slang lexicon as an insult aimed at all manner of imbeciles, idiots, and stupid people. As a result Mike's use of it seems entirely appropriate for Troy and James.

N

NEEDFUL THINGS

Needful Things is a 1991 horror novel written by Stephen King that was the last full-length story to be featured in the author's fictional setting of Castle Rock. The story follows a mysterious curiosity shop which gives the book its title, and which serves as the catalyst to tear Castle Rock apart.

The novel was actually the inspiration behind *Stranger Things'* name. The Duffer Brothers had originally titled their series 'Montauk' after the Long Island town where it was initially supposed to be set. But when the production shifted locations, they also had to change titles, a decision they have described as extremely difficult given their affinity with their original choice.

And like so much of what we see on screen in *Stranger Things*, the twins looked to their childhood influences for inspiration.

'When we were selling it, we made a fake Stephen King paperback cover for the show,' Matt Duffer revealed in an interview with the *Daily Beast*. 'We actually used the *Firestarter* paperback and put our title and an image of a fallen bike on top of it, so when we were trying to come up with titles, we would type them out onto this paperback cover and it would help us. And *Stranger Things* sort of sounds like *Needful Things* – it sounded like it could have been a Stephen King book from the '80s.'

NETFLIX

Originally launched in 1997, Netflix started life as a DVD rental business before expanding into online streaming in 2010. Since then it has grown exponentially and started producing its own original content in 2013. With critically acclaimed shows including *House of Cards* and *Orange is the New Black* under its belt, Netflix began giving opportunities to new producers, providing up and coming talent with an opportunity to showcase their work. It was that mandate that gave *Stranger Things* its big break.

The Duffer Brothers' attempts to pitch their series to the major US networks had been unsuccessful, with many of them rejecting the show on account of its child stars. The studio suits at the big networks believed that audiences would struggle to identify with the young stars and advised the creators that they should either adapt it into a children's show or focus solely on Hopper's paranormal investigations, without the children. Sticking to their original plan, however, the brothers began working with producer Shawn Levy who secured a meeting with Netflix in order to pitch the series.

'Literally Netflix was the first buyer we pitched to,' Levy told entertainment industry bible *Variety* in an interview in 2016. 'By the next morning they bought the season. They were the first pitch because they were our first choice. A big part of that is the Duffers are new and emerging filmmakers and they really didn't want the show to conform to increasingly obsolete notions of what is TV. They always spoke of it as an eight hour movie. It's why they laid hands on every script. It's why we directed all of them ourselves. We wanted a continuity of authorship. And Netflix was our dream home because a) they genuinely empower creative, that's their rep and it's the truth, and b) we wanted people to have the option of watching a big chunk of episodes in a row without having to wait.'

The show first became available to stream on Netflix on 15 July 2016 and instantly became a hit for the streaming giant. Netflix doesn't release viewing figures for its content but analytics companies have estimated that more than 8.2 million people watched the show during the first sixteen days of its release. If those numbers are true it would make *Stranger Things* one of Netflix's most popular pieces of original content, elevating it above the likes of *Orange is the New Black*, *House of Cards*, *Narcos*, *Daredevil*, and *Making a Murderer*.

Considering its success it is perhaps no surprise that Netflix rapidly green-lit a second season for *Stranger Things*.

NIGHTMARE ON ELM STREET, A (1984)

Wes Craven's 1984 slasher didn't just bust blocks at the box office; it was groundbreaking too. The film spawned a procession of sequels, spinoffs, and imitations but it also helped to change how audiences viewed cinema as it blurred the lines between what was real and what was not. The Duffer Brothers have admitted that the frightening figure of Freddy Krueger was one of the films that helped to shape them in their formative years, so its influence on *Stranger Things* should come as no surprise.

Eleven's interaction with the Monster while in sensory deprivation is certainly one aspect that echoes Freddy Krueger's nightmarish attacks on Elm Street's adolescent residents, but perhaps its most notable influence on the fictional events in Hawkins is thematic. In fact the Duffers have repeatedly stated in interviews that they were drawn to the ordinariness of Elm Street, that Craven set his slasher against a backdrop that was instantly recognisable to viewers and then threw a nightmarish curveball into the mix. There's certainly a similar set up to *Stranger Things,* with the nostalgic eighties trappings of suburban America providing a familiar backdrop into which the Duffers Brothers introduce an almost inexplicable evil.

O

OA, THE

Debuting on Netflix in December 2016, *The OA* is a sci-fi show that is the brainchild of Brit Marling and Zat Batmanglij. The series centres on a girl who returns after being missing for seven years in what she claims was an alternate dimension.

Many people have drawn parallels between *The OA* and *Stranger Things*. After all, they both have alternate dimensions, secret labs, strange experiments and unexpected friendships. Indeed the show's creators are friends with the Duffer Brothers and have admitted in interviews that *Stranger Things*' unique brand of smart science fiction influenced their work. Many reviewers picked up on the influence. In *Vanity Fair* Hillary Busis wrote: '*The OA* is, well, stranger than *Stranger Things*. The latter is a loving homage to a bygone era, and especially the movies that it spawned; the former is a lot more unclassifiable.'

The show no doubt reflects the impact of *Stranger Things*' success on the industry. But *The OA* is not only thematically similar to *Stranger Things* – it also contains a nice hidden message for its Netflix neighbour. In its fourth episode, eagle-eyed fans may have noticed that *Stranger Things* is actually playing on the screen as the characters watch TV. The footage is from the *Stranger Things* pilot episode, clearly showing Will Byers, and providing fans of the show with a nice connection to 2016's other big TV sci-fi smash.

O'BANNON, DAVID

Played by Ron Roggé, David O'Bannon is the name of the State Trooper who purportedly found Will Byers' body in the Hawkins town quarry. O'Bannon's name is announced on the news after Byers' body is discovered and the audience is left to surmise that he was instructed by Hawkins Laboratory to report the discover of Will's body in the quarry and to not let anyone else get too close to the cotton-wool stuffed corpse.

O'Bannon's involvement in the discovery of Will's body makes Hopper uneasy, and the Chief questions what a State Trooper was doing dredging up a body in an area that was under his jurisdiction. Intent on getting answers Hopper heads to the bar where O'Bannon drinks and attempts to question him about the discovery. After the State Trooper refuses to co-operate Hopper assaults him in an alley behind the bar-room building, though he refuses to say who he was working for. He then shows his fear of the 'bad men' by telling Hopper he was 'going to get [them] both killed' before running away.

The character's name is one of the many subtle references hidden in the first season of *Stranger Things*. He is named after Dan O'Bannon, the screenwriter of sci-fi epic *Alien* as well as a writer/actor in John Carpenter's 1974 sci-fi comedy *Dark Star*; both of which have been cited as influences by the show's creators.

P

PAPA

Papa is the endearing term that Eleven gave to Dr Brenner during her time under his control at Hawkins Laboratory. It is unknown whether the white-haired scientist made the telekinetic child use the patriarchal term as another form of control, or whether it demonstrates some kind of genuine affection between the pair. It's certainly emphasised throughout the show, though, and only adds to the creepy nature of *Stranger Things*' arch-villain.

As a maniacal scientist who is intent on playing god – even going so far as to fake a boy's death and kill to keep his work a secret – it is well within the realms of possibility to imagine Dr Brenner wanting to take credit for Eleven's amazing powers. However, the term's repeated use has forced fans to speculate over who Eleven's real father is. After all, during Hopper and Joyce's visit to the Ives household we learn that the now-catatonic Terry was pregnant during her time in the Project MKUltra program. The timeline, however, remains unclear. Was she pregnant before she started the experiments – and if so, who is the baby's father? Or, more maliciously, did Terry become pregnant during her time in the top secret CIA program?

The mystery will no doubt be central to the series as it unfolds in season two and beyond, but that hasn't stopped fans from having their say on who Eleven's father really is. One particularly interesting school of thought suggests that the Monster is actually Eleven's father, and that it somehow impregnated Terry Ives during her time in sensory deprivation.

This theory points to the Duffer Brothers' love for the movie *Alien*. In Ridley Scott's sci-fi spectacular one of the most horrific acts in the Xenomorph's catalogue of stomach-churning behaviour, is their violation of the human body in order to reproduce. The end result is obviously the chest-popping spectacle that the movie has become famous for, but the idea of using a human body as a vessel for some kind of parasitic pregnancy also sticks particularly prominently in film fans' consciousness. Given *Stranger Things'* repeated nods towards the sci-fi classic – particularly the slugs, eggs, and spores we see in the Upside Down – it's easy to see why so many Internet comments have been dedicated to the idea of the Monster somehow impregnating Terry Ives, imbuing her future child with some of its powers in the process.

PEANUTS

Charlie Brown is as much a part of a North American Christmas as turkey, presents, and gaudily decorated houses. So given *Stranger Things*' success it was perhaps only a matter of time before someone decided to mash up the much-loved animated character with the residents of Hawkins, Indiana. That someone was YouTube user OnlyLeigh who combined *Stranger Things* with the perennial holiday classic *A Charlie Brown Christmas* for a special Christmas clip.

The three-minute video re-imagines the characters of Hawkins, Indiana as Charlie Brown-style characters, sketching them out in the same rough form that the kids' classic has become famous for. The video picks up straight after the events of the first season with Will Byers taking on the mantle of Charlie Brown. Feeling blue after surviving the Upside Down, he turns to his friends for help. First he visits Linus, recast as the curly-haired figure of Dustin Henderson, and then he sees Eleven who is manning Lucy's Psychiatry Booth from the *Peanuts* universe. Joyce responds to her son's sadness with the wordless 'wah wah wahs' voiced by Charlie Brown's teacher, and finally there is Snoopy himself who is more bloodthirsty monster than man's best friend. There's even an animated dance number set to *Stranger Things*' instantly familiar synth-laden score.

The video became a viral sensation on its release on 27 October 2016, attracting more than 1.8 million views on YouTube.

PHYLLIS

She may be unseen, but lunch lady Phyllis from Hawkins Middle School is responsible for the stash of pudding cups that Dustin finds when the squad set up a sensory deprivation tank in the gymnasium.

POINT AND CLICK GAMES

Point and Click titles like *Escape from Monkey Island*, were a fixture of the video game scene of the 80s and 90s. These games were like interactive versions of *Choose Your Own Adventure* books, where players could interact with the game's environment and cast of characters by clicking on various items on the screen.

Given the nostalgia which seeps from every scene of *Stranger Things* it was perhaps only a matter of time before someone turned the events of the first season into one of these retro styled games. Produced by indie games developer Infamous Quests, the *Stranger Things* point and click game was a demo that was released for free online in August 2016.

Featuring a fully playable level, players took on the

role of Chief Hopper investigating the disappearance of Will Byers in the woods of Hawkins. Like games of the original era players could interact with their environment in order to gather clues, and they could also interact with other characters including police officers Powell and Callahan who would often give irreverent responses.

'I grew up in the 80s – I was younger than the kids in the series, but my older brother was the same age as the characters in 1983, and he was my hero when I was a kid, so I really identified with that,' Steven Alexander, writer and programmer of the game, told *Wired* magazine in an interview in 2016. 'We were always riding our bikes around town, getting into trouble, I played Dungeons and Dragons when I was older, and so on.'

POLTERGEIST (1982)

Along with *E.T.* and *The Goonies*, *Poltergeist* is perhaps the largest big screen influence on the action we see in *Stranger Things*. Written and produced by the Duffer Brothers' muse, Steven Spielberg, the movie was a critical and commercial smash hit that won three Academy Awards and went on to be a key film in the horror genre. More than thirty-five years after its original release, *Poltergeist* is considered one of the best horror movies of all time; it even featured in the American Film Institute's '100 Years...100 Thrills' countdown, which looked back at some of the scariest moments ever to grace the silver screen.

The movie follows the bizarre events that beset the fictional Freeling family in Orange County, California who move into a home that, unbeknownst to them, was built on a plot where a cemetery was once located. All manner of supernatural occurrences then follow, including the family's daughter Carol Anne communicating through TV static, before being dragged through a portal by a 'Beast' from an alternate dimension.

It's a premise that is also seen in *Stranger Things*' first season. As in *Poltergeist*, a family's youngest child is dragged through a portal and held in an alternate dimension by a vicious Monster. Similarly, the story revolves around a mother frantically trying to find their child and even finding a way to communicate with them through the walls of their building.

The parallels don't stop there either. Will's use of electrical currents, including the fairy lights and telephone, echo the TV static in *Poltergeist* which Carol Anne Freeling uses to communicate with an alternate dimension. Just as in *Stranger Things*, the little girl's connection with the other side opens a portal between dimensions leading to all manner of supernatural shenanigans. The scene where the government scientist Shepard is tethered to a cable line and sent through the Gate to the Upside Down as well as Joyce and Hoppers' quest to rescue Will, also directly reference the movie.

If those nods were too subtle, the Duffers offer us a more overt reference to the 1982 scare story in the very first episode. During a flashback Joyce remembers surprising Will with tickets to see the movie itself, even though he would have been too young to watch it.

POWELL

Played by Rob Morgan – the actor who played Turk in another Netflix hit, *Daredevil* – Officer Powell is a member of Chief Hopper's police department in Hawkins. The character appears in every episode of the show's first season and is regularly used in the main plotlines. It is Powell who gives us an insight into Hopper's dalliances with drink and drugs after he and Callahan find the Chief after his first run in with the clandestine team at Hawkins lab. In addition, he accompanies Hopper when he finds Will Byers' bike and also when he uncovers the evidence of Project MKUltra at the Hawkins Public Library.

POWERS

Though the boys say that Eleven has 'Jedi powers', her abilities in *Stranger Things* have nothing to do with the Force. Instead, as we learn from flashbacks to her time under the control of Dr. Brenner they have been carefully honed by the insidious agents at Hawkins Laboratory.

But just what is Eleven able to do?

Early on we see her telekinetic abilities. Telekinesis is the ability to move physical objects with the mind and the shaven-headed girl demonstrates this ability throughout the season. From turning electronic devices off to slamming the basement door so that the boys can't tell Mike's parents of her existence, she is shown to be able to manipulate physical objects with her thoughts. Through flashbacks we are shown that her powers were developed at a young age, able to crush Coke cans and snap her guards' necks – just with the power of her mind.

As she is exposed to the outside world, however, her powers continue to strengthen and develop. At one point she is able to manipulate Troy's internal organs, forcing the school bully to wet himself against his will. Later when he catches up with the boys at the quarry she uses her powers to levitate Mike after he is forced to jump at knifepoint. Her telekinetic powers reach their peak, though, at the conclusion of the first season when she flips a van full of Hawkins Laboratory agents in one of the most spectacular scenes from the show's first season. Later, when attacked at the school by a small army of agents as well as the Demogorgon, she is able to fend off her human attackers by snapping their necks. Not even the Monster can compete with these abilities: she forces it back, pins it against the wall and seems to destroy it.

Alongside her telekinetic powers, Eleven is also shown to have psychic abilities. While she can't read minds quite yet, she is able to eavesdrop on a Russian agent from her sensory deprivation tank in Hawkins. She also demonstrates the ability to access other dimensions, whether it is transporting her consciousness to the Upside Down in order to locate Will and Barb, or using radio equipment to contact the missing Hawkins boy.

Despite the awesomeness of Eleven's abilities, though, *Stranger Things* shows us that using them takes a physical toll on her. Her nose bleeds every time she exerts her powers, a sign of the physical and psychological strain that they place upon her.

Though the boys themselves equate her powers to the Jedi Knights that inhabit the world of *Star Wars,* a more appropriate comparison might be found in the comics that Dustin barters with Will in the very first episode. A group of super-powered mutants with an array of abilities, the X-Men are one of Marvel Comics' most famous titles. One of their leading characters is Jean Grey, a mutant with telekinetic and psychic abilities that are not unlike those that Eleven possesses.

PORTALS

The main connection between Hawkins and the Upside Down is the Gate, which was created by Eleven's contact with the Monster during a failed experiment in one of the subterranean basements at Hawkins Laboratory. But, besides the Gate, a number of Portals between the two dimensions open up throughout *Stranger Things*' first season. Unlike the Gate these Portals aren't permanent, but more like temporary tears in the fabric between dimensions that seal up in time.

Though it is unknown what causes these Portals, the fact that they coincide with attacks by the Demogorgon suggests that the Monster can in some way create them. The audience see these Portals in episodes four and five when Nancy and Jonathan stumble across the monster feasting on a deer in the woods. Following the trail of blood left by the carcass, Nancy stumbles through a Portal to the Upside Down. This gooey gateway is almost organic in nature, a membrane of sorts that separates the two dimensions in much the same way as the Gate does.

PROPS

From calculator watches and walkie-talkies to wall-mounted telephones and period-appropriate cars, the props in *Stranger Things* play an important role in creating a believable setting for Middle America in 1983. Prop master Lynda Reiss was the woman tasked with building this world around which the action revolves. Reiss is no stranger to high profile projects having worked on movies ranging from *American History X* to *American Beauty*. Handed a $220,000 budget she was tasked with tracking down items that were near-antique, uncovering long-forgotten gems that would help to add texture to the show's period setting.

Everything from the characters' wardrobe to the folders they carry to school had to be sourced with Reiss, who insisted that her department find original items rather than recreate them. 'I don't want to do a nostalgia-tinged product,' Reiss told *Wired* magazine in an interview. 'I want it to be the '80s. I don't want it to be what everyone just thinks is the '80s. Our baseline was the reality of the midwest in 1983.'

In order to find the items she took to online sites such as eBay and scoured flea markets and estate sales in Atlanta. Even members of the production crew contributed their own personal effects, such as the Dungeons & Dragons rulebooks you see on the screen, in order to make the props as period-appropriate as possible.

Despite their best efforts the props department weren't able to source original versions of all of the props. Often this was an issue caused by the nature of the script which required several of each item so that they could be destroyed or used in stunts. Notable items that needed to be recreated included the boys' bikes, which were carefully crafted and aged to make them look like they had come straight out of the early 1980s.

As well as sourcing the props, Reiss has revealed in interviews that she actually had to educate the show's young cast on how to use many of them. After all, many cast members weren't even born when these items were originally in use, and had no idea how to interact with them. On one occasion, Reiss remembers, an actor needed to use a wall-mounted telephone. 'He comes over and picks up the phone and is yelling, "Hello! Hello! Hello!" and pressing the buttons,' she told CBC Radio. 'I said, "No, in 1983 you would've pulled the handset holder up and down to get a line out."'

Though the prop department's work has been widely praised for authentically recreating Middle America in the early 80s, not all items featured on screen have met with universal acclaim. With viewers who fondly remember the period in which the show is set, many people have been quick to point out potential inaccuracies. Some of those include Barb's car, a version of the Volkswagen Cabrio that wouldn't have been released until 1988. Likewise the Demogorgon figurine that the boys use to illustrate the Monster wasn't actually available for Dungeons & Dragons players to buy until after 1983.

These inaccuracies were among those parodied by internet comedy site CollegeHumor whose mock video 'What Year is "Stranger Things" Set in?' has attracted more than 750,000 views on YouTube.

PUDDING

'Mike! I found the chocolate pudding!', or so Dustin excitedly exclaims after uncovering Hawkins Middle School's secret stash of chocolate pudding that was squirrelled away by lunch lady Phyllis. Complete with Dustin's trademark grin, it's one of the most memorable moments of the first season

The chocolate puddings in question are Hunt's Snack Packs, which were first introduced in North America in 1969. Sold in packages of four cans, the Snack Packs were self-contained desserts designed to take advantage of the packed lunch market, and to this day they remain a staple of America's brown bag brigade. Originally packaged in aluminum cans, the product was swapped into plastic containers in 1984 – partly because of the number of people who cut their tongues on the can in a desperate bid to lick the last morsels out of an empty container. As a result the stash of cans that Dustin uncovers in Hawkins circa 1983 would have been one of the last lots of canned pudding available.

Obviously the prop department couldn't locate original tins of the pudding for the show so they produced their own retro labels and fixed them on cans of Vienna sausages, which the young cast members found disgusting when they opened them.

The appearance of the pudding in *Stranger Things*' first season – complete with the original packaging – helped launch a swathe of snack nostalgia across the US. Indeed the company behind the gooey lunchtime staple were reportedly swamped with calls from fans of the show asking Hunt's to bring back the early 80s metal packaging. The demand was so great, in fact, that the company is reportedly exploring the potential for a special retro Snack Pack rollout to coincide with future seasons of the show.

QUARRY

The water-filled quarry in Hawkins is owned and run by Frank Sattler, head of the Sattler Company. Aside from its fictional setting, the real-life location for the quarry is actually the Bellwood Quarry in Atlanta, Georgia. It's not the first time this location has featured on our screens either: it previously appeared in *The Walking Dead*, *The Vampire Diaries,* and *The Hunger Games*.

The quarry provides the backdrop for some important action during the first season of *Stranger Things*. It is one of the first locations that Hopper investigates when searching for Will Byers, and later in the series it is where the fake body is discovered.

The quarry is also where Mike, Dustin and Eleven's

final confrontation with Troy and James takes place. Here the bullies confront the boys and threaten to cut out Dustin's teeth unless Mike jumps into the water. It is a fall that would almost certainly kill the young boy – even though, earlier in the series, Officer Callahan spins a tale about local resident George Burness surviving the fall while drunk. But in an act that is testament to the boys' friendship Mike doesn't hesitate to step over the ledge in order to save his friend; he in turn is saved by Eleven's telekinetic abilities before she proceeds to break Troy's arm, in one of the show's most fist-pumping moments.

R

R-RATED

Even though the show is filled with young actors and
1980s adolescent nostalgia, *Stranger Things* visits some
pretty dark places during the first season. Yet in the
original drafts of the show's script, the action went even
further. The Duffer Brothers revealed, on the red carpet
at the 2017 Golden Globes, that their original vision was
more R-rated, with far more violence than we got to see
in the final version.

'The Eleven character, the kind of powers she has
and to have a young protagonist that's violent – it's not
E.T. It's not a happy situation. She's killing people, and
brutally murdering them,' Ross Duffer told red carpet
reporters. 'The original pilot was much more violent. It
was originally like an R-rated thing.'

However Eleven's actions weren't the only thing to be toned down before the series debuted on Netflix. In the same red carpet interview Matt Duffer also revealed that Joyce Byers, played by Winona Ryder, was also far more potty-mouthed than the finished product would have us believe. 'Winona's character was like, "Eff this, eff that!"' he said. 'It felt a little bit unnecessary. I don't feel like we sacrificed anything by toning it down a little bit.'

For those not in the know, the R rating is the Motion Pictures Association of America's rating for 'Restricted Viewing', roughly equivalent to a UK 18 rating, suggesting that the show contains adult material.

RATINGS

It's hard to gauge the ratings of Netflix shows in the same way as mainstream series that appear on the broadcast networks. After all Netflix releases all episodes of a season at once, enabling viewers to watch them at their own leisure. Most series are also released with little fanfare, with the video streaming giant instead preferring titles to gain traction through word of mouth and social media buzz. Finally Netflix has a policy of not releasing their viewing figures to the public.

So how do we know how successful *Stranger Things* has been?

Thanks to a tech company called SymphonyAM, which uses Netflix ratings to estimate viewing figures, we have some idea of the show's success. SymphonyAM released data in August 2016 that showed the extent to which *Stranger Things* had taken off. In the first 35 days after Netflix made season one of the show available, an average of 14.07 million adults between the ages of 18 and 49 had watched it on the streaming service.

To put that number into some kind of context it sets the series above the likes of *Making a Murderer* (13.35 million), *Daredevil* season two (13.35 million), *Jessica Jones* (6.26 million), and *House of Cards* season four (5.67 million) in terms of ratings. In fact, if SymphonyAM's figures are correct, it would make *Stranger Things* the third most successful series in Netflix's history, with only *Fuller House* and season four of *Orange is the New Black* attracting a larger audience in their first 35 days of streaming.

ROANE COUNTY CORONERS

Roane County Coroners run the morgue in downtown Hawkins, where Will Byers' fake body is taken after it is discovered in the quarry. The staff at the morgue comprises the coroner, who is called Gary, his unnamed assistant who was played by director/producer Shawn Levy, and a receptionist called Patty. Jonathan and Joyce Byers are initially called to the coroners to identify the body in episode four, but Joyce refuses to believe that it is her son. This helps to fuel Hopper's suspicions and lead him to break into the morgue and discover that the body was indeed a fake.

RUSSIAN AGENT

In episode five of *Stranger Things'* first season we get a glimpse of what the CIA would probably do with Eleven's psychic abilities. Dr Brenner uses her to literally listen in on the conversation of a Russian agent, before broadcasting it over Hawkins Laboratory's loudspeaker system. The flashback sequence shows us the type of experimentation that Eleven was subjected to during her time in incarceration, and also serves as a precursor to further experiments that would lead to her meeting with the Demogorgon and the opening of the Gate to the Upside Down.

However, when Eleven does listen in to the Russian agent there are no English subtitles, so what exactly does the man say? Sadly for those of you who are looking for some kind of hidden message that would shine a light on the dark dealings of Dr Brenner and the Hawkins team, his statement is far more benign. Roughly translated, the Russian agent is warning his counterpart that their spies have been exposed by the Americans and implores him to bring the operatives to him so that he can get to the bottom of the issue.

RYDER, WINONA

Born on 29 October 1971, Winona Ryder, is undoubtedly the most established star in the *Stranger Things* cast. Named after the town of Winona, Minnesota where she was born, her upbringing, as part of a literary family, saw her move around a lot, from farms in the Midwest to communes in California. For much of her formative years she lived with no TV or movies but became an avid reader and an ardent fan in particular of J.D. Salinger's novel, *The Catcher in the Rye*.

Ryder developed her love of acting aged ten after her mother showed her some movies on a screen at the family barn. Aged twelve, she enrolled in the American Conservatory Theatre in San Francisco where she took her first acting lessons. Her big break followed soon after when she taped herself reading a passage from Salinger's novella, *Franny and Zooey*, and sent it to director David Seltzer. Seltzer, who was casting for a movie called *Desert Bloom* at the time, took note of her talent and signed her on to appear in his next project, *Lucas*. Released in 1986 the coming-of-age drama also starred Corey Haim, Charlie Sheen and Kerri Green. It was a moderately successful movie but one that would significantly set the young starlet on the course to international fame.

Critical acclaim came with Ryder's next screen appearance, in 1987's *Square Dance*, but it was her turn in *Lucas* that caught the eye of director Tim Burton who decided to cast her as the goth teen Lydia Deetz in his iconic dark comedy *Beetlejuice* (1988). The film was a box office smash hit, and launched Ryder into the public and critical consciousness..

She next starred with Christian Slater in *Heathers* (1988), then a box office flop, but one that would later go on to achieve cult status and cement Ryder's spot as one of Tinseltown's most prodigiously talented teens. Her agent reportedly begged her not to take the role of Veronica Swayers for fear of ruining her career. It's easy to see why, given the film's macabre subject matter about an outcast and her offbeat boyfriend killing off popular kids at their suburban high school. Critics liked it, though, with one *Washington Post* reviewer describing her as 'Hollywood's most impressive ingénue…'

Heathers set the tone for a string of critically acclaimed Ryder performances in films like *Great Balls of Fire!*, *Edward Scissorhands*, *Dracula*, and *Mermaids* – for which she was nominated for a Golden Globe for Best Supporting Actress. For *The Age of Innocence* and *Little Women*, she received Oscar nods for Best Supporting Actress and Best Actress respectively.

The good times wouldn't keep on rolling for Ryder however as she went on to star in a series of limp films that flopped spectacularly at the box office. Though she was lauded for her performances, films such as *Boys*, *Looking for Richard*, *Crucible*, and *Alien: Resurrection* would see her stock drop on the silver screen. Things went from bad to worse for the actress in 2001 after she was arrested and convicted of shoplifting for stealing $5,500 worth of luxury designer goods from Saks Fifth Avenue department store in Los Angeles. Her conviction became the talk of the tabloids with Ryder's depression and prescription drug use taking centre stage, and would lead to a hiatus from Hollywood.

Finally, in 2010 Winona Ryder made a remarkable comeback, as Spock's mother in J.J. Abrams' *Star Trek* reboot, before appearing in box office successes like *Black Swan*, *The Iceman*, and *Frankenweenie* which saw her reunite with director Tim Burton.

During this time Ryder also found fame on the small screen, scoring a Screen Actors Guild nomination for her turn as the titular character in CBS's made-for-TV biopic *When Love Is Not Enough: The Lois Wilson Story* (2010). Five years later she was back on television with a much-praised portrayal of Vinni Restiano in HBO's *Show Me a Hero* before finally finding her way to *Stranger Things*.

Winona Ryder was one of the first names suggested by casting director Carmen Cuba and it was an idea the show's creators instantly fell in love with. They weren't the only ones, though: her appearance also attracted the attention of fans. After all, casting an eighties icon in a series set in the eighties seems like the perfect piece of meta-casting. But Ryder brings so much more than nostalgia to the role. Indeed she isn't just an eighties icon, she is the *right* eighties icon; a kooky, eerie presence who fits perfectly with the outsider tone of the series.

The Duffer Brothers explained their decision to cast Ryder during an interview with *Vulture* in 2016. 'Certainly there's nostalgia there, but this is someone we were huge fans of growing up, and it's someone we just wanted to see more of,' Ross Duffer said. 'And it's particularly someone we loved seeing in the supernatural genre. Not that she's not great in other things, like *Girl,*

Interrupted or *Little Women*. But Tim Burton was such a huge inspiration to us growing up and those movies were such a part of our rotation. It was also assigning us the idea of putting a movie star in this role because we always saw this as a big eight-hour summer movie. So to have someone like Winona, who has that movie-star presence where you just point a camera at her and she pops off the screen, it's not something most people have. So we were excited by the idea of her doing this. And I don't think even two years ago she would have agreed to it. I do think Matthew McConaughey and his McConaissance was a huge help and opened up the door to some of these people that are more traditionally known for film.'

Like so many of the other actors in *Stranger Things*, Ryder signed onto the series on the strength of just one script, and so the Duffer Brothers were able to tailor the role of Joyce Byers to her. Originally Byers was meant to be a foul-mouthed Long Island mother with a tough exterior, but Ryder's anxious energy prompted the writers to mould the role around her, transforming her into the emotional centre of that first season. Ryder herself, meanwhile, helped to shape how Joyce would look. It was Ryder's idea, for instance, who suggested her character's hair should look like Meryl Streep's in the 1983 movie *Silkwood*.

For Ryder there was a lot of emotional weight tied up in the role of Joyce Byers. In 1993 she had been heavily involved in the search for a missing twelve-year-old girl by the name of Polly Klaas, even offering a $200,000 reward for her safe return. Klaas, who lived in Ryder's former hometown of Petaluma, California, was kidnapped at knifepoint from her home and later murdered. Ryder dedicated her role in *Little Women* to Klaas's memory as it had been the girl's favourite book.

'I've seen first-hand that tangible grief, you can literally feel coming out the pores of the parents,' Ryder told *Time* magazine in an interview in July 2016. 'Not that I would ever use that. I kept that separate. I'm still very close with her family. But I think it's the worst thing you can ever experience as a parent.'

Ryder's performances provided some of the standout moments of the show's first season. Critics singled her out for acclaim. Reviewing the series for *Variety*, Maureen Ryan noted: 'Winona Ryder, whose tightly coiled intensity effectively anchors the series, is one of its most retro aspects... Ryder has a number of solo scenes in which odd and possibly supernatural things happen to her or her home's appliances, and in the wrong hands, the scenes might have seemed faintly ridiculous, or clichéd. But her passionately committed performance and quicksilver versatility make those moments not just scary but, at times, even moving.'

Ryder was a regular on the red carpet following the show's success, scoring Best Actress nominations at the Fangoria and Saturn Awards. But it was at the Screen Actors Guild Awards in early 2017 when she once again hit the headlines. Nominated for Outstanding

Performance by a Female Actor in a Drama Series, she also joined the rest of the cast on stage as they accepted the gong for Best Ensemble Cast. Though David Harbour took centre stage for his politically charged acceptance speech, it was Ryder's bizarre string of facial expressions that caught people's attention, becoming one of the most talked-about memes on social media following the awards.

S

SCHAPP, NOAH

Born in New York in October 2004, Noah Schapp plays Will Byers on *Stranger Things*. Though it has made him a star, the series isn't his first screen appearance – in 2015 he played Tom Hanks' son in Steven Spielberg's movie *Bridge of Spies*, and shortly afterwards followed that up by voicing the character of Charlie Brown for *The Peanuts Movie*.

Off of the back of these appearances, in 2015 he went on to audition for *Stranger Things*, but initially read for the roll of Mike rather than Will. In 2016, speaking about the casting process to *The Hollywood Reporter* he said: 'I definitely remember that it was a long process, the auditioning. At first I went as a normal audition into this casting office, and I originally auditioned for the role of Mike (Finn Wolfhard). But when I got my callback later on, they asked me to play for Will… They told me that I got the role while I was at camp. Honestly, when my parents called me, they were like, "We have someone on the phone for you." And I was like, "Who is it?" And they were like, "It's the Duffer Brothers, those people from *Stranger Things*!" I thought they were lying. They told me I got the role, and it was crazy. I was in camp, and I was just so excited.'

Given his previous work with Spielberg, Scnapp was perhaps an ideal choice for a series that plays so much homage to the great director, citing key films like *E.T.*, *Jurassic Park* and *Schindler's List* as inspirations for him.

Despite his success, however, Schapp has kept his feet firmly planted on the ground; he still rides the bus to school, for example, and attended classes even whilst filming for the first season of *Stranger Things* was taking place.

He also credits Winona Ryder for the impact she had on him and the other kids during filming. Speaking to *Entertainment Tonight* in September 2016 he said: 'Well, first of all, she was always helping me. And she was always looking out for me. I remember in episode eight, she was with me when we were doing a CPR scene: She gave me gum and she put gum in her mouth and she looked me in the eye and said: "So our breath doesn't smell bad." Because she had to put her mouth on my mouth. And I also remember her talking to my mom to make sure I was OK for that scene when David Harbour [Chief Hopper] had to really push hard on my chest. Honestly, she was amazing.'

After working on the first season of *Stranger Things*, Schapp returned to the silver screen for indie flick *We Only Know So Much*, based on an Elizabeth Crane novel, and which also stars Jeanne Triplehorn and Damian Young. He will return for the second season of *Stranger Things*, as the show continues to explore what happened to his character during his time in the Upside Down.

SEASON TWO AND BEYOND

Stranger Things season two was confirmed by Netflix on 31 August 2016. Netflix confirmed the return of the show in a tweet which simply read: 'The adventure continues.' Netflix also confirmed that the cast of the first season would be returning to the show, with newcomers Sean Astin, Sadie Sink, Dacre Montgomery, and Paul Reiser joining the cast. Soon after this, the video streaming service released the Chapter titles for season two's episodes, and an air date of 31 October 2017 was announced during an advert at halftime in the 2017 Super Bowl. In July 2017, this was brought forward a few days to 27 October.

Even before they'd started shooting on season two, the Duffer Brothers were already working on storylines for further seasons, with plans to continue the show for up to five seasons in total. 'I want it to have a really finite ending," Matt Duffer told *Entertainment Weekly* in 2016. 'I don't want it to be one of those shows that runs out of gas, and they lose it because they're losing interest. You wanna end when you're on top.' To which Ross Duffer added: 'Hopefully. you'll come to the end of Season 2 and feel fully satisfied and want more, but you'll feel like it has come to a conclusion. But also we've laid the ground work for further seasons.'

Production of the second season officially got underway on 2 November 2016 when the cast returned for table readings of the Duffers' scripts. Netflix captured the moment on social media. A black and white photo featuring the cast along with their scripts was posted the wrong way up, in reference to the Upside Down, alongside a caption which read: 'Back in production ... see you next year ...'

Fans had to wait until July 2017 for their first real look at the on-screen action however, with Netflix keeping footage from season two carefully under wraps before releasing a feature-length trailer at the San Diego Comic Convention.

Set to the ominous voiceover from Michael Jackson's 1984 smash hit 'Thriller', the trailer is crammed full of the usual period trappings ranging from retro arcade games to Ghostbusters Halloween costumes. But the three minutes of footage doesn't just tease more of what we saw in the show's first run, it sets up a second season that promises to be altogether more ominous than its predecessor.

The trailer focused heavily on Will Byers, suggesting

the boy who escaped from the Upside Down will play an integral role in the events of season two. That's if he ever actually fully escaped the Upside Down, as the trailer shows several shots of the alternate dimension bleeding into the real world in much the same style as the bathroom scene that ended the first season.

Indeed it seems that the side effects of his time spent in the Upside Down are only getting worse and we catch glimpses of a nightmarish vision of Hawkins that's been entirely annihilated by a giant monster. Whether this is a vision of the future, a flashback to what caused the desolation that we see in the Upside Down, or an example of the increasing blurring of the boundaries between the two dimensions remains to be seen.

The trailer also seemingly answered one of the biggest questions fans had following the finale of the show's first season, that being whether Eleven would return. During its closing moments the teaser gives us our first glimpse of everyone's favourite telekinetic child since she disappeared following that climactic clash with the Demogorgon at Hawkins Middle School. Dressed in the same outfit as when we last saw her, it looks like Eleven has survived the encounter but somehow found herself trapped in the Upside Down. Thankfully it looks like she might be set to return to Mike and his squad, as the trailer ends with her finding a new portal back to Hawkins.

SHEPARD

Played by Christopher Cody Robinson, Shepard is the name of a Hawkins Laboratory employee who is sent through the Gate by Dr Brenner. Wearing a Hazmat suit and tied to a winch, he is the first person to travel through the Gate after it forms following Eleven's interaction with the Demogorgon.

Reporting back through the Gate via radio he screams as he is attacked by the Monster, shouting 'There's something else in here! Pull me out! Pull me out, pull me out! Pull me out! Pull me out!' The laboratory team attempted to winch Shepard back in as the sound of the Monster played over the intercom but all that came back through the Gate was the chain and a bloodied piece of Shepard's Hazmat suit.

In some places the character is credited as Test Pilot Shepard which has led many to believe that the character is a nod towards Alan Shepard, who was the first American in space. The character has also been the centre of many fan theories thanks to the fact that Dr Brenner refers to him as 'son'. Given the fact that Eleven calls the white-haired scientist Papa, this has led people to surmise that Shepard may be another number from the Project MKUltra program, or indeed Brenner's actual son, although neither theory has been confirmed.

'SHOULD I STAY OR SHOULD I GO'

Originally recorded by The Clash in 1982, 'Should I Stay or Should I Go' is a punk anthem and a favourite song of Jonathan and Will Byers. In a flashback we see that Jonathan shared the song with his younger brother so that it could help to shield him from their parents' arguments during their divorce. It's often featured during the season, appearing at key moments: Will sings it to himself in the Upside Down, as a way to comfort himself while trying to evade the Demogorgon. The song is also played on the stereo by Will as he attempts to communicate through electricity from the other dimension.

SLANG

From its Dungeons & Dragons figurines, to its wood-panelled cars, and period-appropriate clothing; everything that we see on screen in *Stranger Things* is deliberately chosen to fit in with its 1980s setting. But how period-appropriate are the vocabularies of the show's characters? After all, all of its period trappings would count for nought if the script had its teens conversing like smartphone-wielding, Internet-literate millennials.

Fortunately the show doesn't fall into this trap, and like every other aspect of its production there are signs that the show's creators have paid careful consideration to how real life teens would have talked to each other in the Midwest during the 1980s. The word 'douchebag', for example, is thrown around during the opening episodes, no doubt a nod to the term's growing popularity among eighties teenagers following its appearance in films like *Revenge of the Nerds* and on the popular *Saturday Night Live* skit Mr and Mrs Douchebag. Hawkins teenagers sprinkle their conversations with words like 'cool', 'chill' and 'gross', and whilst they seem to be ever-present in adolescent vocabularies, they naturally fit in with the show's 1980s setting. The same can be said for terms like 'mouth breather' and 'wastoid', which the squad fires around at their Middle School tormentors. 'Wastoid' in particular has a distinctly 1980s flavour to it, as is proved by its use in the 1985 classic *The Breakfast Club* when Andrew tells Bender, 'Yo wastoid, you're not gonna blaze up in here.'

SNOW BALL

The Snow Ball is a festive dance that takes place each year at Hawkins Middle School. Mike calls the dance 'cheesy' and admits that he's never attended it before, but for the 1983 event still asks Eleven to accompany him as his date. His request is a signal of the romantic bond that is developing between the two, but unfortunately Eleven disappears before the ball begins.

SOUNDTRACK

As much a part of the show as Dungeons & Dragons, kids on bikes and sinister government organizations, the soundtrack of *Stranger Things* turned out to be one of the series' most surprising stars, and as a whole feels much more than a collection of 1980s pop oldies and sinister synthesiser scores. Featuring the likes of The Bangles, Toto, Jefferson Airplane, Peter Gabriel and Foreigner it features some of the biggest bands of the time; the kind of stuff that the kids of Hawkins, Indiana would have been listening to before their lives were interrupted by a bloodthirsty Demogorgon.

The Duffer brothers have admitted that as unashamed movie nerds, music wasn't exactly their strong suit; so instead of plucking tracks from their own memories, they meticulously worked alongside Music Supervisor Nora Felder to pick the right tune for the right moment.

'For us, we didn't Tarantino it – it's not like this stuff was written in the script,' Ross Duffer said in an interview with *Complex*, referring to Hollywood director Quentin Tarantino's penchant for structuring his movies around songs from his own record collection. 'The Clash's "Should I Stay or Should I Go?" was planned, but all the other stuff... it was more us listening to as much Eighties music as we could and seeing what hit the right mark. It was definitely trial and error. Obviously, we played around in terms of what would actually be played around 1983 – for us, it was more about the tone and the feel, and the stories these songs were telling.'

Despite the hit parade of 1980s classics that feature in *Stranger Things*, pop music is just one part of what makes the show's soundtrack tick. The other is the electronic synth music that sets the tone right from the opening credits. Like so much of the series, the soundtrack recalls classic 1980s films that inspired it, such as John Carpenter's eerie scores for films like *Halloween*. But more modern influences crept in too: inspired by Nicolas Winding Refn's 2011 cult hit *Drive*, and the moody ambient sounds that landed David Fincher's *The Social Network* an Oscar for Best Original Score at the 83rd Academy Awards, the Duffer brothers hired Texan band S U R V I V E to provide the other half of the show's soundtrack.

Indeed even before they'd secured a deal to produce their series, the Duffers were using S U R V I V E's work to set the tone for *Stranger Things*, using a track called 'Dirge' to score the mock trailer they produced for studio execs. So the band's involvement was almost inevitable when the series was green-lit by Netflix. Getting in on the ground floor enabled the band to produce the show's soundtrack while scripts were being written and actors were being cast in key roles, instead of just adding music after the action had already been shot. As a result their music is interwoven into every aspect of the action.

'We had a few scripts, but we were pitching the demos before they had even finished casting,' S U R V I V E's Kyle

Dixon told *Pitchfork*. 'They played some of the demos that we had done against the auditions, so I think the music kind of informed who they cast, and vice versa.'

In total S U R V I V E produced more than fourteen hours of score material, so it was no wonder that they had to spread the soundtrack across two volumes when it was eventually released to the public during the summer of 2016. Nor was it a surprise when the soundtrack started to attract critical acclaim, with each volume landing individual nominations in the Best Score Soundtrack category at the 2017 Grammy Awards.

SPECIAL EFFECTS

Like everything else on *Stranger Things,* the special effects used in the show were developed through a period of careful consideration by its creators. In an age where CGI special effects are commonplace on the small screen it could have been easy for the Duffer brothers to rely on technical wizardry in creating the world of their hit series. But instead, they once again leaned on their formative years and the practical effects that helped to make eighties movies such a success.

Looking back at movies like *Hellraiser*, *Alien,* and *The Thing*, the Duffer Brothers wanted to create that sense of authenticity by producing the first season of their show using nothing but practical effects. It's an admirable idea. However, the realities of modern production quickly forced them to use some CGI during their first season.

'The funny thing is that the original goal was to do entirely practical effects,' Ross Duffer told the *Daily Beast*. 'But what we realized – and it really made us admire those guys who did *The Thing* and *Alien* and whatever – is that doing practical is really hard. It takes a lot of time and preparation. We were turning out scripts as quickly as we could but they don't have six months to prep this stuff. You show up on set and stuff that seemed like it would be a great idea to do in that old school way, we didn't have time to do.'

The brothers have admitted that, despite their best efforts, at the end of the first season the balance between practical and modern computer-generated special effects was about 50/50. Nevertheless, that's still an impressive ratio for a modern production. It's also noticeable that some of the most iconic moments from that first season are actually those that were created with old-school practical effects.

The scenes where Eleven enters the void after being placed in sensory deprivation are a prime example. These abstract sequences take the viewer inside the telekinetic girl's mind, showing us her encounters with the Demogorgon and her exploration of the Upside Down. For these scenes the Duffer Brothers could have resorted to CGI but instead embraced the limitations of practical effects. In order to create the isolation effect they filled a set with a small pool of water, and surrounded it with black curtains. It's a simple enough idea that ends up becoming one of the most powerful images in the series.

The brothers have stated in interviews that they took their cue for these sequences from Jonathan Glazer's 2013 science fiction film *Under the Skin.*

The sequences in the void weren't the only areas where the use of practical effects paid off. Much of what we see of the Upside Down, for example, was also created through on-set production design. The vines and goo coming out of the Gate in Hawkins laboratory was all created on set, while prosthetics were used to create Will's fake body and the decomposing corpse of Barb which is seen during the series finale. Indeed the Duffers only resorted to using CGI for the Upside Down when they had to shoot entire streets.

Perhaps the most iconic effects used by the brothers during the show's first season are those used to create the Monster itself. 'It has always been something of a lifelong dream to create a monster and bring it to life on-screen. Not in the computer, but for real,' the Duffers wrote during an episode recap on EW.com. 'To build it. Like so many filmmakers our age and older, we grew up on genre films that existed before computer graphics. There was something about the effects being so tangible in those films that made them especially terrifying to us when we were kids. We're specifically thinking about Ridley Scott's *Alien*, John Carpenter's *The Thing*, and Clive Barker's *Hellraiser*. So from very early on we knew we wanted to build an animatronic monster.'

That monster was created by LA-based special effects company Spectral Motion, who are best known for producing the effects on Guillermo del Toro's *Hellboy* franchise. The end product, a suit that was operated by performance artist Mark Steger, took about two months to create. The suit weighed 30 pounds and contained more than 26 motors, which were so loud that Steger couldn't hear what people were saying on set. Steger walked on eight-inch metal stilts to give the monster its terrifying height, whilst puppeteers controlled the Demogorgon's gangly limbs via remote control. The end result was so plausible that some of the children on set were scared of Steger when he was in his suit, and the production team had to reassure them that he was a good monster, like the kind they'd find in *Monsters Inc.*, in order to calm them down.

SPIELBERG, STEVEN

Even among the kaleidoscope of pop culture influences that can be seen in *Stranger Things*, Steven Spielberg stands out as the most important. The director's career has been a clear influence on the Duffer Brothers with films like *E.T.*, *Poltergeist* and *Close Encounters of the Third Kind* all referenced during episodes in the first season.

Spielberg himself needs very little introduction. With a career spanning four decades on the silver screen the director's resume reads like a greatest hits of cinema's best blockbusters. And even though he has recently helmed Hollywood smash hits like *War Horse* (2011),

Lincoln (2012) and *Bridge of Spies* (2015), it's the earlier chapters of Spielberg's career that have the most notable impact on *Stranger Things*.

The key word in Spielberg's earlier work is escapism. Films like *Close Encounters of the Third Kind* (1977) and *E.T: The Extra Terrestrial* (1982) focused heavily on science-fiction, but other flicks such as *Jaws* (1975), *Raiders of the Lost Ark* (1981) and *Poltergeist* (1982) continued his obsession with all things strange. These films also set out many of the tropes which you can see bleeding into the world of Hawkins.

The idea of incredible events unfolding in the altogether more mundane surroundings of suburban American is a popular Spielberg theme, one that played out in films like *The Goonies* (1985), *E.T.* and *Poltergeist*; and which is also a heavy influence on the events of *Stranger Things*. Closer inspection, though, reveals a smattering of other Spielberg inspirations. Whether it's the idea of kids being chased by mysterious men in cars, parents willing to go to any length to rescue their children or the overwhelming optimism of an outsider, these emblems of Spielberg's work can be seen in almost every episode of the show.

'Steven Spielberg films were huge touchstones for us growing up,' Matt Duffer told the *Daily Telegraph*. "We wanted to evoke the sense of wonder we remember from our childhood, from *E.T.* and from Stephen King novels."

Alongside the thematic influences of Spielberg on *Stranger Things*, there are also more overt references in the series to his work. Look closely and you'll spot a *Jaws* poster in Jonathan's bedroom, whilst the scene where the monster attacks Barb after she bleeds in the waterappears to be a reference to the aquatic classic. There are also more *E.T.* references than you can shake a bag of Reece's Pieces at, with Eleven's makeover, the van flip scene and the boys riding around suburban Middle America on their bikes all evoking the iconic eighties Spielberg flick. Elsewhere Joy's obsession with fairy lights offers a neat callback to *Close Encounters of the Third Kind*, whilst her obsessive pursuit of her son is almost certainly influenced by *Poltergeist*. Throw in a childhood adventure (*The Goonies*) and a sensory deprivation tank reference (*Minority Report*) and you can see how the action is punctuated by constant nods to one of the Duffer Brothers' favourite movie makers.

STAND BY ME (1986)

Directed by Rob Reiner, *Stand by Me* was based on a Stephen King short story called 'The Body'. Starring Will Wheaton, River Phoenix, Corey Feldman and Jerry O'Connell the coming-of-age drama follows four boys from small-town Oregon who, while on a hike, discover the body of a missing child. Critically acclaimed and commercially successful the film helped to launch the careers of its child stars but also became a barometer by which all future child-starring films would be measured.

As the Duffer Brothers were fans of Stephen King,

it's perhaps no surprise to learn that they were heavily inspired by the film. During the casting process of *Stranger Things*, they even got the boys in their cast to read passages from its script, in order to assess their onscreen chemistry. *Stranger Things* also shares similarities with *Stand by Me*. For instance, when Eleven leads Dustin, Lucas and Mike on a walk along the train tracks as they attempt to find Will, it recalls a similar scene in Reiner's movie. *Stranger Things* also borrows tonally from the flick: the group of boys are carefree, living innocent lives founded on their friendship before they are exposed to profound tragedy and loss that ultimately strengthens the bonds between them.

In an interview with *Variety*, Matt Duffer addressed the comparisons: 'We always wanted to keep the stakes high. When you're looking back at *Stand by Me*, the stakes feel very real. The kids never feel completely safe, even though there is an element of fun and you love those boys. There's this consistent danger with Kiefer Sutherland coming after them, the train coming so close to them – we wanted to always keep the kids in real danger, that's not "Dungeons & Dragons" danger.'

In an interview with *TheWarp*, Will Wheaton – who played Gordie in Rob Reiner's film – called the show's homage 'an incredible honor', and 'one of the greatest things I've ever experienced in my life as an audience member'. In the same interview Wheaton pointed to the similarities between the Duffer Brothers' exhaustive casting search in order to find its squad of boys and the one conducted by Rob Reiner in 1986. 'It's what makes something like *Stranger Things* so wonderful and so rewarding and so memorable,' he said.

'We get to see actors who we've never seen before just become these roles,' he added, speaking of the young *Stranger Things* cast members. 'We can embrace the characters and they become real the same way the characters in *Stand by Me* did for our generation.'

STEGER, MARK

Born on 16 January 1962, Mark Steger is an actor and performance artist who was cast to bring the *Stranger Things* Demogorgon to life. Wearing a suit created by LA-based production company Spectral Motion, Steger was responsible for the practical effects seen in the show's first season.

But the man inside the monster is no stranger to the screen. Steger has a career that stretches back almost three decades with performances in movies like *I Am Legend* and *The Last Witch Hunter*, together with small screen work on the 2008 miniseries *Heroes: Going Postal*.

STUFFED TOY THEORY

When is a stuffed toy more than a stuffed toy? When it's in the hands of a *Stranger Things* fan, of course.

The stuffed toy theory began to circulate after eagle-eyed fans of the series spotted the same kind of plush toy owned by three of the key characters. But could a stuffed toy really be the key to unravelling *Stranger Things*' secrets? The answer, amazingly, could be yes.

In the first season we can see that Eleven, Will, and (in flashback) Hopper's now dead daughter Sarah all have the same childhood toy, a stuffed animal that appears to be some kind of tiger or lion. The toy can be seen in Eleven's cell in Hawkins Lab, in Castle Byers with Will, and in a flashback hospital scene with Sara. It's a small, possibly inconsequential detail, but given the amount of effort that the Duffer Brothers have put into every other aspect of their show it seems deliberate. But what does it mean?

Online fans have theorised that the toys link the three characters somehow, which suggests that Will and Hopper's daughter might have powers similar to Eleven's. It also suggests they might even have been a part of Dr Brenner's nefarious experiments at some point or other. Could that explain how Will manages to survive for so long in the Upside Down? Does that mean that Hopper's daughter is actually dead, or was her death part of a cover up?

Of course there could be a more mundane explanation: maybe the props department just used a particular brand of toy, or the stuffed animals may be the mascots of nearby school sports teams. But whatever the case it's an interesting idea, and fans have committed thousands of words to discussing it on Internet forums.

SUPER BOWL

Netflix aired the first trailer for *Stranger Things* season two during the halftime show of the 2017 NFL Super Bowl, in one of the most prestigious advertising slots in television, watched by millions around the world. Even though Netflix were competing in that break against more than sixty-five major brands, *Stranger Things'* retro-themed trailer attracted the most attention on social media. It topped the audience interaction charts according to data released at the time by monitoring firm iSpot.tv. In fact it attracted more than three times the Twitter traffic of the next highest advertiser with more than 307,000 Tweets during the game's broadcast.

S U R V I V E

Comprising Michael Stein, Kyle Dixon, Adam Jones and Mark Donica; S U R V I V E is an experimental synth-heavy electronic quartet from Austin, Texas. Originally formed in 2009, the band's first EP entitled *BATH017* was released in 2010. Since then they have produced a further four EPs and three albums. Their debut album *Mnq026* was released in May 2012 and featured the single 'Dirge', which the Duffer Brothers featured on *Stranger Things'* fake trailer in order to pitch the series to studios. In September 2016, a new album called *RR7349* was released to critical acclaim.

Despite almost a decade in the industry S U R V I V E

had to wait patiently for their big break. This came in 2014 when their track 'Hourglass' made it onto the soundtrack for Adam Wingard's horror flick *The Guest*. The movie itself wasn't all that successful but the band's inclusion on the soundtrack did attract the attention of the Duffer Brothers who were working on creating their high-concept TV show at the time.

The band's career skyrocketed along with the success of the show. They were able to quit their day jobs and embark on a North American tour, got nominated for two Grammy awards, and were even invited to create the music for an immersive restaurant experience in Australia. Talk about overnight success!

T

TANGERINE DREAM

Founded in 1967 the prolific electronic pioneers Tangerine Dream, from Berlin in Germany, have released more than one hundred albums to date. They've also had a significant impact on the music industry and popular culture, helping to inspire the kind of synth-heavy sound that is instantly recognizable on *Stranger Things*. As well as inspiring the sound of the series – Texan band S U R V I V E have cited the band as a key influence on their work for the series – three Tangerine Dreams tracks actually feature on the soundtrack of episodes five, six and eight: respectively, the title tracks from the albums *Green Desert* (1986) and *Exit* (1981), and 'Horizon' from their 1984 album *Poland*.

The German synth masters' association with the show came full circle when the band released their own 21st century take on the *Stranger Things* soundtrack. The haunting synth-track was made available on SoundCloud where, since its release in September 2016, it has been listened to more than 200,000 times.

TATTOO

Eleven, the shaven headed hero of *Stranger Things'* first season, is so named after Mike sees '011' tattooed on her forearm. The tattoo, though, turns out to be a brand, another example of the horrific treatment that Millie Bobby Brown's character has received at the hands of her 'Papa', Dr Brenner, at Hawkins Laboratory.

Eleven has been thrown in a windowless cell and submitted to terrifying experiments, but '011' also symbolizes shows that she has been stripped of her humanity – just another number to the nefarious organization.

But is there more to Eleven's numerical name than meets the eye? After all, why choose '011'? Why not '001' or '004'? The number raises the interesting prospect that Eleven isn't the first graduate of Hawkins Laboratory's Project MKUltra and that others have gone before her, ten of them to be precise. The idea is heartbreaking, that other children were subjected to the secret testing of the 'Bad Men'. But it also raises the interesting question of what happened to those other victims? Are they still alive? Are they stationed at other facilities? Do they have the same powers? Or have all of them died after over-exerting their powers?

THE THING (1982)

Among John Carpenter's seminal slasher films and creepy horror classics, *The Thing*, starring Kurt Russell, has a special place in the hearts of the Duffer Brothers. A loose remake of the 1952 B-movie, *The Thing from Another World*, Carpenter's film observes an isolated Antarctic outpost that becomes targeted and overrun by a parasitic organism from another planet. Full of brooding claustrophobia and paranoia it's one of the moodiest movies of the decade, and even more than 35 years on from its original release its influence still resonates, thanks largely to its eye-popping special effects.

Its impact on *Stranger Things* can be seen first and foremost in the Duffer Brothers' desire to use practical effects wherever possible. Though they had to resort to using some CGI imagery the Duffers used production designers to create the series' Monster as well as physical aspects of the Gate and the Upside Down. Speaking to the *Daily Beast* in 2016 the brothers underlined their appreciation for Carpenter's movies: 'Those guys in *The Thing*, not only does that stuff hold up, it looks real. There's something tangible about it and it's not an easy thing to do, so those guys are our heroes.'

The Thing's influence on the Duffer Brothers' series

goes beyond its use of special effects. There's a poster for the film hanging in the basement of Mike's house for example – though how the teenage boys got to see such an adult movie is a question for their parents to answer. The film is referenced once again when Dustin calls Mr Clarke to ask about building sensory deprivation tanks. As the phone rings the science teacher is shown to be watching the film at home alongside his girlfriend.

THESSALHYDRA

The Thessalhydra is a Dungeons & Dragons figure that appears during the final episode of the show's first season. This enemy features in the quest that the crew completes on Christmas Eve 1983, bookending the action with the Dungeons & Dragons game they attempt during the opening episode.

Just like their first on-screen adventure, the boys are confronted with a final foe as Mike summons the fearsome Thessalhydra at the end of their ten-hour quest. Unlike their battle with the Demogorgon, though, this time the party vanquish their foe, with Will the Wise fireballing the 'son of a bitch'. After the beast falls to the ground Lucas's knight chops off seven heads which Dustin's dwarf puts in a bag to present to King Tristan for their prize.

Just like the Demogorgon, the Thessalhydra is an actual Dungeons & Dragons character that would have been available to gamers of the era. It first appeared in 1983 and was one of a series of Thessalmonsters that were designed and not born. The beast resembles the many-headed serpent from Greek mythology, but there are some key differences. Instead of multiple heads sprouting from a reptilian body the Thessalhydra's heads all form a ring around a large circular mouth that's lined with razor-sharp teeth and can spit acid. The tail is also different and ends in a set of pincer-like teeth.

Apart from being period-appropriate the Thessalhydra could also prove important to the *Stranger Things* universe. After all, the appearance of the Demogorgon seemed to foreshadow the events that took place in season one, so it is perhaps unsurprising that fans leapt on the Monster's appearance. Many speculated that the fact the Monster was designed and not born was noticeable, given Dr Brenner's tinkering with Eleven. Eagle-eyed fans also noted that Will's crew only lopped off seven of the monster's eight heads during their Dungeons & Dragons quest. It might seem an insignificant detail, but given that the in-game monster can regenerate if any of its heads aren't destroyed – and in some iterations reproduce by infecting hosts – it suggests that the boys have been too quick to celebrate their victory of the Demogorgon, a point that seems to be reinforced when Will coughs up an Upside Down slug during the series' final scenes.

TELEPHONES

The Duffer Brothers' original script called for *Stranger Things* to be set in 1981, but one of the things that made the brothers change their mind about the show's timeline was the humble telephone. The issue was that the USA's Bell Telephone Network wasn't officially broken up until 1982, which meant that Americans didn't actually own their own phones. Had the action in Stranger Things taken place in 1981, then when Joyce Byers fried her phone attempting to contact Will, she would have had to wait for the telephone company to come to replace it. Keen to ensure the authenticity of their show the Duffer Brothers worked with prop master Lynda Reiss to find out when homeowners could start buying their own phones, and adjusted the timeline accordingly.

TROY

Played by Peyton Wich, Troy is the resident bully of Hawkins Middle School. A weapons-grade douche who takes pleasure in teasing Mike, Dustin and Lucas he is one of the minor antagonists of *Stranger Things*' first season. Friends with his fellow bully James, Troy confronts Mike and his crew in the very first episode, teasing and tormenting them by wondering which one would do best in a freak show.

Thereafter, Troy only becomes more unlikeable, showing no sympathy towards the boys after the disappearance of their friends and even tripping Mike up in the schoolyard, causing him to cut his chin. Later in the show's first season his behaviour becomes even more despicable: he confronts Mike and Dustin at the quarry armed with a knife. Angered after an incident at a school assembly when Eleven made him wet himself, Troy captures Dustin and threatens to cut his baby teeth out unless Mike jumps from the top of the quarry.

Eleven once again comes to Mike's rescue however, using her powers to break Troy's arm. It's some welcome comeuppance for a character who plays the role of pantomime villain in the show, and one who will no doubt return in future seasons to provide some social injustice for our geeky heroes.

TWITTER

It's the 21st century so it's no surprise to see that the cast of *Stranger Things* are active on social media. Indeed the vast majority of the show's actors have accounts, and regularly take to Twitter to express their feelings in 140 characters or less.

The key accounts to follow, to keep up to date with *Stranger Things* on Twitter, are:

Official account – @Stranger_Things
Millie Bobby Brown (Eleven) – @milliebbrown
Gaten Matarazzo (Dustin Henderson) – @GatenM123
Noah Schnapp (Will Byers) – @noah_schnapp
Finn Wolfhard (Mike Wheeler) – @FinnSkata
Caleb McLaughlin (Lucas Sinclair) – @calebrmclaughl1
Charlie Heaton (Jonathan Byers) – @CHeatonOfficial
Joe Keery (Steve Harrington) – @joe_keery

STRANGER THINGS A-Z

Natalia Dyer (Nancy Wheeler) – @NataliaDyer

Shannon Purser (Barbara Holland) – @shannonpurser

David Harbour (Chief Hopper) – @DavidKHarbour

Cara Buono (Karen Wheeler) – @CaraBuono

Matthew Modine (Dr Brenner) – @MatthewModine

Randy Havens (Mr Clarke) – @MrRandyHavens

Ross Partridge (Lonnie Byers) – @PartridgeRoss

Peyton Wich (Troy) – @PeytonWich

Chelsea Talmadge (Carol) – @ChelseaTalmadge

Chester Rushing (Tommy H) – @ChesterRushing

U

UPSIDE DOWN

The Upside Down is the alternate dimension that exists throughout the first season of *Stranger Things*, although it is never explicitly stated what the realm actually is. Is it an alternate universe, another reality, a dimension? It is never actually made clear. It is also unknown whether the Upside Down has always existed or whether it only came into being after Eleven made contact with the Demogorgon during season one.

Indeed so much of what we know is hypothetical, whether it is in Mr. Clarke's theories about alternate dimensions or Hawkins Laboratory's knowledge of the gateway in their sub-basement. Even the name isn't real, it's the name given to the dimension by the boys after Eleven tries to explain Will's whereabouts to them using the flip side of a Dungeons & Dragons board.

Much of what we know about this alternate dimension comes from our own exposure to it as viewers. Initially that comes via snapshots: when Barb is snatched from the bottom of the pool for example, or when Nancy inadvertently gets pulled through a rift in the woods. Our only sustained exposure to the realm comes during the series' denouement when Hopper and Joyce enter the Upside Down in search of Will. Even then, however, Hopper's words as he and Joyce approach the Gate echo the mystery that shrouds the alternate dimension. 'Everything that's happened here, and everything that's going to happen, we don't talk about,' Hopper intones. 'You want Will back? This place had nothing to do with it. That's the deal. Got it?'

What we do know about the Upside Down is that it appears to almost exactly replicate the human world, containing the same locations and geography as the town of Hawkins itself. The space also appears to share similar physics. Gravity exists there, for example, as well as an atmosphere and visible light. There are some key differences, though. For starters, the Hawkins Laboratory staff members confirm that the atmosphere appears to be toxic, although judging by Will's survival its effect takes time to impact on the human body.

The Upside Down also appears to be overflowing with organic matter. The air is laden with thick white spores, for instance, while every other surface is overgrown with tendrils, roots and vines. The surfaces are also sticky to the touch, covered with a kind of thick mucus which is perhaps best exemplified when the dimension comes into contact with the real world. The Duffer Brothers have said during interviews that they wanted this rift to be disgusting, like a membrane or something biological rather than the kind of portal you would typically find in science fiction.

The biological matter isn't all plant-based, however; as poor Barb knows only too well, there is life in the Upside Down too. The Monster is obviously the prime example of this, and the design of the Demogorgon is very much in keeping with its surrounding universe. But as we see during the show's finale it is not the only thing that lives beyond the Gate. We briefly see an alien egg as Hopper and Joyce attempt to search out Will. We also get to witness a slug-like creature emerge from the missing boy as Hopper attempts to resuscitate him.

As you might imagine from the show's meticulous creators, every aspect of the Upside Down was carefully considered. During the development phase, the Duffer Brothers turned to Aaron Sims Creative, who also helped to produce the design for the Demogorgon in order to visualize the Upside Down. Their brief, like so much of their universe, took inspiration from popular culture, notably the organic nature of the Xenomorphs in the *Alien* films and the ash-laden dreariness created in the popular video game series *Silent Hill*. That ash imagery in particular can be seen in the spores that clearly differentiate the Upside Down from reality.

Using the brief from the Duffer Brothers the artists at Aaron Sims Creative searched out their own inspiration. They didn't research any scientific theory, though, instead relying on more obscure areas to spur their communication. One starting point was mould and the process of decay in nature, helping to inspire the image of the Upside Down as a world that is dead, or in the process of dying. They also found inspiration in the work of Polish artist Zdzisław Beksinski. Speaking during an interview with Screencrush in 2016 Aaron Sims said:

'More specific influences came from the art of Polish painter Zdzisław Beksinski, whose paintings felt slightly hellish. They reflect an otherworldly, hellish world, surrounded by a thin layer of something we can't quite make out. They're terrifying, and were definitely an inspiration for our work here.'

However, not every idea cooked up during its conceptualisation made it into the first season of *Stranger Things*. For example the initial designs for the Upside Down painted it as a far more colourful place, filled with bright light. Another idea that failed to make it onto our screens is that there was a time difference of sorts between the Upside Down and the real world. In fact during initial concepts when it was night time in the real world, it would have been day time in the Upside Down and vice-versa.

Even though we only get to scratch the surface of the Upside Down during the first season, you can rest assured that future installments will continue to expand on what we know about it.

'There's a lot there we don't know or understand,' Ross Duffer confirmed during an interview with *Variety*. 'Even with the Upside Down, we have a 30-page document that is pretty intricate in terms of what it all means, and where this monster actually came from, and why aren't there more monsters – we have all this stuff that we just didn't have time for, or we didn't feel like we needed to get into in season one, because of the main tension of Will. We have that whole other world that we haven't fully explored in this season, and that was very purposeful.'

'THE UPSIDE DOWN'

'The Upside Down' is the title of the season one finale of *Stranger Things*. It is directed by the Duffer Brothers, who also wrote the episode with help from Paul Dichter. The episode brings to a climax many of the adaptive strands from the first season as Joyce and Hopper set off into the Upside Down to save Will.

Once they are inside we are treated to our most intensive exposure to the alternate dimension, as they search for and find Will in the Hawkins Library. The episode also finally fully reveals the Demogorgon, as Jonathan, Nancy and later Steve do battle with it in the Byers household. Later we see it in all its gory glory as Eleven goes toe-to-toe with the Demogorgon after fighting the 'Bad Men' at Hawkins Middle School.

The episode itself ends in a cliffhanger designed to lead into season two of the show. First we jump four months into the future where Will has recovered from his ordeal and is back among his friends enjoying another quest of Dungeons & Dragons. Just like the first episode the action appears to foreshadow what we might expect from the show's return as well as poking fun at the loose ends of the show's first run.

Those loose ends include Hopper, who is shown to be in cahoots with the sinister Hawkins Laboratory. It's not all bad for our favourite hat-wearing law officer, however: he ends the episode leaving a box of Eggos out in the forest for Eleven, who hasn't been seen since the incident at Hawkins Middle School.

Overall the tone is incredibly light, a neat and tidy ending wrapped up in the festive spirit of the season. But just when we think the show will serve up something of a happy ending, the tone shifts with Will excusing himself from the dinner table to go to the bathroom. Once there he coughs up a slug from the Upside Down. The critter slithers down the drain as the camera pulls back to reveal the boy inside the alternate dimension, suggesting that all is not well as the first season comes to a close.

V

VALE OF SHADOWS

The Vale of Shadows is another Dungeons & Dragons reference to feature in *Stranger Things*' first season, and another way that the boys refer to the Upside Down when Eleven reveals that it is there where Will is being held. It's an accurate reflection of the Upside Down as we know it, especially later in the season when Joyce and Hopper enter the dimension to find it is an almost exact replica of real life Hawkins, only somehow contaminated with gloom, organic matter and all kinds of vines.

Though there is no actual Vale of Shadows card within Dungeons & Dragons, the reference does seem to hark back to Shadowfell, otherwise known as the Plane of Shadows, which appeared in the fourth edition of Dungeons & Dragons.

As well as serving to help audiences (and the boys) better understand the Upside Down, the Vale of Shadows also tees Mr Clarke up for one of the fan favourite character's knock-out lines during the first season. 'You know the Vale of Shadows?' Dustin asks at Will's wake, a somewhat geeky question that would probably be met with a blank look and a confused response by any other adult in the show. However Mr Clarke isn't any other adult and without missing a beat he begins to answer before Dungeon Master Mike stops him mid description. It's a wonderful moment for the character, and one which only emphasises the connection he has with his students.

VAN FLIP

Episode seven of *Stranger Things* features perhaps one of the biggest action set pieces during its entire first season. The stunt itself comes during the bike chase when Mike and his friends are attempting to outrun the 'bad men' from Hawkins Laboratory, who have managed to track them and Eleven down.

The scene itself is comparable to the infamous bike chase scene from *E.T.* which the Duffer Brothers have readily cited as one of their biggest influences. However, unlike Steven Spielberg's adorable alien, the BMX-mounted crew don't escape their pursuers by taking their rides airborne. Instead, appropriately in the altogether murkier world of *Stranger Things*, the action is a little more intense as Eleven uses her telekinetic powers to flip the Hawkins Laboratory van that is attempting to block the bikers' path.

Speaking during one of their episode roundups on EW.com, the Duffer brothers described the sequence as one of their favourite moments from the first season, but one that was difficult to achieve.

'The van flip was a lot of fun...' they wrote. 'And very stressful.'

Just like they had with the Monster and the Upside Down, the brothers wanted to perform the van-flip stunt using practical effects rather than CGI wizardry. The plan was to film a separate shot of the flipped van to intersect with the chase scene. However the producers insisted they couldn't flip a van that high into the air. Nevertheless, after some insistence on the part of the show's creators and a successful test, the stunt was set to go ahead. However not everything went as planned when they stepped onto the set.

Indeed on the day of shooting the van stunt one of the explosive charges that was set to propel the van up and into the air failed to go off. No one was hurt but the mishap caused the van to skid headfirst into one of the crew's cameras, destroying it and in the process costing the production several thousand dollars. The setback once again prompted the producers to try and call a halt to the stunt, but upon the insistence of the Duffer Brothers they attempted it for a second time and captured the stunning shot which played an important part in both the series and its promotion.

'THE VANISHING OF WILL BYERS'

'The Vanishing of Will Byers' is the name of the first episode of the first season of *Stranger Things*. Written and directed by the Duffer Brothers, this pilot episode is the only script they had completed when the show was green-lit by Netflix.

The episode itself welcomes viewers to the world of Hawkins, Indiana. It starts with some frantic action in the lower levels of Hawkins National Laboratory where a scientist runs for an elevator and frantically begins pushing the buttons, before being violently jerked upwards by something above him. Meanwhile the boys are playing Dungeons & Dragons, with their fight against the Demogorgon foreshadowing the events that would unfold throughout the series. As the episode title suggests, much of the action revolves around the mysterious disappearance of Will Byers. However it also neatly introduces us to many of the debut season's principal characters including Joyce, Jonathan and Chief Hopper. The episode also sets up the relationship between Steve and Nancy and, perhaps most importantly, gives us our first glimpse of Eleven.

VOID

Some of *Stranger Things'* most visually arresting sequences take place in the Void, the dark expanse that Eleven visits when she is placed in a sensory deprivation tank. The Void represents the young girl's psychic abilities – it's a dark vacuum that connects the real world from the Upside Down. The Void is a kind of gap between the show's dual dimensions, one which is populated by elements from each but doesn't truly exist in either.

In the show the Void is depicted as a huge expanse of nothingness, a dark space that's filled only with a thin pool of water and whatever it is that Eleven's mind is focused upon. Eleven can only enter the space when she is deprived of her senses, such as when she is submerged into the deprivation tank in Hawkins Laboratory, or when she is lowered into the makeshift rig that Dustin sets up in the school gymnasium. By shutting down her other senses she is able to create mental projections which can be used either to observe or interact with other people.

We first see the Void in a flashback when Dr Brenner is putting Eleven's abilities to the test. Lowering his charge into a custom-built sensory deprivation tank, Eleven enters the Void and is able to locate and eavesdrop on a Russian spy broadcast his words over the lab's loudspeakers. The experiment demonstrates the extent of Eleven's powers as she is able to project her mind across the other side of the world, but it also gives us a clue as to the dangers that exist in the Void as she hears a growling from a sort of creature that spooks the girl into aborting the experiment.

Despite being reluctant to find out about the source of the sound, Eleven is coaxed back into the sensory deprivation tank by Dr Brenner, who wants her to re-enter the Void and make contact with the creature that she heard in there. What results is one of the spookier sequences of the series: Eleven finds the Monster which appears to be hunched over and feeding on one of the large eggs we'd later see in the Upside Down. She is cautious, but urged on by her 'Papa', Eleven makes contact with the Monster, causing a rift to form between reality and the Upside Down and unleashing the Demogorgon onto the unsuspecting residents of Hawkins.

During the resulting chaos Eleven escapes, and she does not re-enter the Void until asked to help contact Barb and Will in the Upside Down. After her experience with the Demogorgon she is clearly scared to go back to that space. However Joyce comforts the girl, showing her genuine tenderness and support as she attempts to find the missing duo. At first Eleven is spooked as she locates the gruesome sight of Barb's body. Thanks to Joyce, however, she is calm enough to continue – she finds Will hiding from the Monster in Castle Byers and relays Joyce's message that she is coming for him and to hang on until she can get there.

The Void is an abstract way to demonstrate Eleven's abilities, but it's not the first time we've seen this kind of visual representation of psychic powers in popular culture. Thanks to the recent rush of comic book movies we've seen all manner of ways of depicting psychic abilities. The most notable example, perhaps, Professor Xavier in the *X-Men*'s various incarnations. Whether he is played by Patrick Stewart or James McAvoy, the shaven-headed psychic's abilities are generally depicted using CGI special effects magic, showing action unfolding in a kind of psychic ether.

It would have been easy for the Duffer Brothers to follow this example, but even for a streaming giant like Netflix the budget for TV shows is only a fraction of those reserved for feature films. As a result they had to get creative with their visual effects and followed the template laid out by Jonathan Glazer's 2013 cult hit *Under the Skin*. The sequences, which are comparable to those featured in the film, which starred Scarlett Johansson; were created using thick black curtains which shut out the light on set. They also covered the floor with a pool of water. Both are relatively simple techniques, but when combined with expert lightning they create the perception that the audience is inside Eleven's mind.

WAYWARD PINES

Wayward Pines is a sci-fi television series that debuted on Fox in March 2015. Set in the mysterious town of the same name, it follows a group of inhabitants who live seemingly idyllic lives even though they are not able to escape the electric fence that traps them in their community. Starring Matt Dillon and Juliette Lewis and executive produced by M. Night Shyamalan the series garnered positive reviews upon its original release, with many calling it a return to form for the director of movies such as *The Sixth Sense* and *Unbreakable*.

However Shyamalan wasn't the only person whose career got a boost as a result of the series: the Duffer Brothers were invited to write for the show after

Shyamalan had seen their movie *Hidden*. Together the brothers contributed to four episodes in season one: 'The Truth', 'Choices', 'A Reckoning' and 'Cycle'.

'That became our training ground, and M. Night Shyamalan became a great mentor to us,' Ross Duffer told *Rolling Stone* when asked about the experience.'By the time we came out of that show, we were like, "OK, we know how to put together a show." And that's when we wrote *Stranger Things*.'

'THE WEIRDO ON MAPLE STREET'

'The Weirdo on Maple Street' is the second episode of the first season of *Stranger Things*. Written and directed by the Duffer Brothers the episode is one of the show's longest, with a running time of over fifty-five minutes.

The action picks up right after the events of the pilot episode with the boys continuing to question the runaway girl Eleven about Will's disappearance. She uses the Upside Down of their Dungeons & Dragons board to show them where their friend is. Meanwhile Joyce continues to frantically search for any clue of her son's whereabouts, pushing Hopper to search for Will while receiving strange calls and electrical signals in her house from someone she believes is her missing son. The episode also marks the last appearance of Barb who, left alone at Steve's house party, is attacked by the mysterious monster that is stalking Hawkins.

The episode title is actually a callback to an episode of

the acclaimed American anthology series *The Twilight Zone*. Originally airing on 4 March 1960 it is one of the most loved episodes of the series and depicts a suburban idyll which deteriorates into violence and suspicion.

WRIST ROCKET

The wrist rocket is Lucas's weapon of choice when facing off against the Demogorgon. The high powered slingshot is an actual brand of catapult, one that would have been aspirational for wannabe warriors in the 1980s. Of course its effectiveness against the Demogorgon is non-existent, as we see during the season finale when Lucas, Mike and Dustin face off against the faceless monster at Hawkins Middle School. It does however prove Lucas's bravery and the lengths he will go to protect his friends.

As well as offering another enjoyable eighties throwback, the wrist rocket is yet another reference to the Duffer Brothers' favourite author Stephen King and his terrifying clown tale, *It* and can be compared to the character of Beverly Marsh whose skill with a slingshot is crucial in the battle against Pennywise.

WOLFHARD, FINN

Born on 22 December 2002, Finn Wolfhard is best known for his role as Mike Wheeler on *Stranger Things*. Raised in Vancouver, Canada – where he still attends Catholic school – Wolfhard is the son of a screenwriter and wanted to act ever since watching Sam Raimi's *Spider-Man* movies. The young star also credits his dad for giving him the acting bug. His father used to watch movies for inspiration whilst he was writing scripts, and almost by default Wolfhard would watch them too, feeding his desire from a young age to work in showbusiness.

Amazingly his first onscreen role came after he replied to an ad on the Internet. 'I got my first gig on Craigslist,' he revealed in an interview with *Dazed* magazine. 'It can be sketchy. But that's how I got my first shot. Then I did an acting class for the summer, but it didn't really help.'

From there his career began to take off. Aged just eleven, his earliest appearances were in little-known indie films called *Aftermath* (2013) and *The Resurrection* (2013), and he also appeared in music videos for the Canadian punk band PUP. His first TV appearance came in 2014 when he guest starred in an episode of American post-apocalyptic drama *The 100*. Wolfhard played the role of Zoran, though you'd be forgiven for not recognising him: he played a nomadic child with a facial deformity, a role that required him to wear make-up and prosthetics. In 2015 Wolfhard appeared in an episode of the long-running hit *Supernatural*, which is shot near his hometown, as well as appearing in local stage productions of Shakespeare plays.

However his biggest break came when he was cast for the first season of *Stranger Things*. Wolfhard was one of hundreds of young actors who auditioned for the role, but unlike many of those who applied he was already well versed in 1980s period detail when he submitted his tape.

'I read the log line from it, which was "An '80s love letter tribute to John Carpenter and Steven Spielberg films." And I was like: "I'm in!"' he told Vulture. 'I grew up watching '80s and '90s movies. I watched *The Goonies*, which is one of the movie this pays inspiration to. And *E.T.* obviously, and *Stand by Me*. It definitely resonated with me right when I read the script.' His love for all things eighties doesn't just stop at moves, though. He is also a big fan of music from that era, counting The Clash, Tears for Fears, and A-Ha among his favourite bands.

When it came to getting the gig on *Stranger Things*, Wolfhard actually sent his audition into the show from his sickbed, filming himself and emailing it to the producers. He received a callback, and proceeded to speak to the Duffer Brothers via Skype before heading to LA to be interviewed in person. There's no doubt that Wolfhard is a star in the making, but he claims that his similarities to the show's creators helped him get the role. 'A lot of the reason was – this is a cheat, but it's awesome – me, Matt, and Ross have so many similarities,' he told Vulture. 'I'm very similar to Matt and Ross, and they kind of wanted to sculpt their past "them" into an actor, if that makes sense at all. We had this running joke on set that I'm basically them as a kid.'

Following his breakout performance in *Stranger*

Things, Wolfhard has been quickly gaining a reputation as sci-fi's newest It-boy, an apt description as he would be cast as Richie Tozier in a remake of Stephen King's *It*. That story of a mysterious evil befalling a sleepy American town treads similar ground to *Stranger Things*, and with good reason. After all King's work has been a key influence on the Duffer Brothers, so much so that they actually vied to work on the *It* remake before starting work on their Netflix series.

With future voice work on an animated series called *Carmen Sandiego*, scheduled for 2019, it seems that the sky is the limit for Wolfhard, and he is already plotting other projects beyond his work in front of the camera. A music lover with a passion for alternative bands of the 1980s and 1990s, he's keen to try his hand at releasing an EP; he's also been inspired by the Duffer Brothers to create his own show and claims he would love to work as a writer/director someday.

WALKIE-TALKIES

They may look arcane by today's standards but the walkie-talkies that Mike and his friends use to keep in touch during the first season of *Stranger Things* would have actually been pretty high-end for the era. With their long antennas and bulky handsets the radios recall iconic 1980s films like *The Goonies*, but they were also commonly available to buy in 1983, when *Stranger Things* is set. The handsets used in the series are actually from a brand called Realistic, which were sold by American electronics giants Radio Shack.

WHEELER, KAREN

Played by Cara Buono, Karen Wheeler is one of the most prominent adult characters during the first season of *Stranger Things*. Mother to Mike and Nancy, she is the archetypal 1980s American housewife, forever fussing over her kids of cooking casseroles to comfort her distraught friends. She is married to Ted, though the marriage is depicted as anything but a happy one – the couple are distant towards each other. Indeed, Nancy says that she doesn't believe that her parents are in love, but instead got married because they were young and Ted had a well-paid job.

At the outset of season one she also has a fractious relationship with her children, particularly Nancy whom she clashes with after she returns late from Steve's party. However she is always shown as a caring maternal influence; she empathises with Joyce's agony over her missing son, comforts Nancy after Barb's disappearance, and does everything in her power to cheer-up Mike – even offering to rent him an R-Rated movie.

WHEELER, MIKE

Though the search for Will Byers triggers the action for *Stranger Things*' first season, it is the character of Mike

Wheeler who represents the show's heart. Played by Finn Wolfhard, the gangly geeky boy is one of the key protagonists – the Dungeon Master through which we experience the adventure.

The middle child of the Wheeler family, Mike has a typical love/hate relationship with his older sister Nancy and a distant one with his parents, whom he doesn't trust with the secrets he learns. Nevertheless he is in essence a good boy, the kind of kid who would forego getting into trouble in order to win science fairs, fiddle with electronic equipment in The A.V. Club, and compete in epic Dungeons & Dragons sessions.

He is defined by his friendships and is a key figure in the group of boys who search for Will Byers. Mike grew up next door to Lucas and the two are best friends, but that friendship is tested with the arrival of Eleven. In a short time (they have only known each other for six days) Mike and Eleven develop a close relationship. It is Mike who decides to take Eleven in and give her food and shelter, and it is also Mike who gets closest to the superpower stranger, teaching her about the world and even eventually inviting her to the Snow Ball.

Mike's relationship with Eleven epitomises the kind of bond he has with those around him. He is sensitive and thoughtful; like the other boys he is a card-carrying nerd but he also understands emotions, as is demonstrated by his nurturing relationship with Eleven or the pain with which he greets the apparent death of his friend Will. He is also bullied at school and alongside Dustin bears the brunt of Troy and James' attentions. The loyalty he displays towards his friends is repeatedly remarkable. Whether it is sheltering Eleven, skipping a curfew to search for Will, or leaping off the quarry in order to save Dustin, nothing is too much to ask from this most committed of characters.

Like the character he plays in Dungeons & Dragons, Mike is the Dungeon Master, the person through which most of the action is experienced. His role as a central character is also reflected in his name, Mike being an apparent nod to Sean Astin's hero Mikey in *The Goonies*.

WHEELER, NANCY

Perhaps no-one in *Stranger Things'* first season undergoes quite the same transformation as Nancy Wheeler. Played by Natalia Dyer she may not have got as much Internet love as her BFF Barb, but she is perhaps just as important – a flawed character who is struggling to find her own identity at an age we can all associate with.

Nancy starts the season as a kind of bookish, all-American girl next door type. She is studious and well liked, and we learn from Dustin's brief interaction with her that up until recently she would have plenty of time for Mike and his friends. However as the action begins to unfold, Nancy begins to change. She has recently entered a relationship with the school's bouffant bad boy Steve Harrington, a popular kid but who seems be outside Nancy's usual social circle.

This burgeoning relationship doesn't go unnoticed, however, as both Barb and her mother express concern for Nancy's newfound association with the cool kids. Barb especially feels uncomfortable about the situation, and is reluctant to accompany her friend to the mid-week pool party held by Steve and his friends. She remains reluctant at the party and wants Nancy to leave with her and go home, but Nancy heads upstairs with Steve, abandoning her friend in favour of her new relationship. This proves to be a watershed moment for the young teen as Barb goes missing after being attacked by the monster from the Upside Down. Realising her decision to let her hormones overrule her relationship with Barb, Nancy begins to take matters into her own hands to find out what happened to her best friend.

This mission leads her into a love triangle with Jonathan Byers, after Nancy realises that he inadvertently captured the Demogorgon on camera when he was peeping in on her and Steve using his camera. Nancy takes control of the situation, hatching a plan to find and kill the Monster by any means necessary. By the end of season one she is a completely different woman to the one who began it, becoming one of the driving forces of the plot's latter stages and solidifying her position as one of the strongest female characters on the show.

WHEELER, TED

Father to Mike and Nancy and husband to Karen, Ted is the bumbling father figure of the Wheeler family. Played by Joe Chrest, he is mostly a minor character in the first season. Indeed he seems oblivious to the strange things that are taking place in Hawkins, a point that is proved emphatically when he says 'This is our government. They're on our side...'

X, Y AND Z

X-MEN

As card-carrying geeks who love nothing more than to waste away their Christmas Eves playing Dungeons & Dragons, it's perhaps no surprise to hear the boys talk about comics in *Stranger Things*' first season. But what you might think of as a throwaway argument about an X-Men comic is actually a very important piece of foreshadowing for the series.

In the opening episode, when they are riding home from Mike's house, Dustin and Will have a wager. The bet involves a race back to their homes and if Will wins he will win one of Dustin's comic books, more specifically Dustin's copy of X-Men issue No. 134. It's the last thing Will says to the audience before getting attacked by the Monster, but the specific issue he mentions is no accidental choice.

Written by Chris Claremont and drawn by John Byrne, X-Men No. 134 was published in 1980 and marks the beginning of what's known as the Dark Phoenix Saga. For comic book fans this is one of the most important issues, featuring one of the most important storylines in the comic's history. The action revolves around Jean Grey, a young woman with psychic and telekinetic abilities who is exposed to cosmic radiation that unlocks the full extent of her powers.

Her newfound abilities do not go unnoticed, though, and a nefarious villain called Mastermind, along with some bad men from a clandestine organisation known as The Hellfire Club, seek to capture her and use her as a weapon for their own gain. In order to control her they use Mastermind's abilities to trap Jean Grey/The Dark Phoenix in a world of illusion, where they test the extent of her abilities. But the Phoenix breaks free from their control and sets about destroying everything in her wake, before finally Jean Grey regains control and, realising the monster she has become, decides to destroy herself, along with the dark power possessing her.

Sound familiar? Compare it with the action that takes place in *Stranger Things*' first season. Eleven is also a girl with telekinetic and psychic powers. She too is manipulated by bad men into using those powers for evil, and she too releases a monster from the darkness. Even the way she exits the show, seemingly destroying herself in an effort to save Hawkins from the Monster she has unleashed, echoes the demise of the Dark Phoenix.

This isn't the only apparent nod to the X-Men storyline, though. The moment when Eleven faces off against the Demogorgon in a Hawkins Middle School classroom, pinning the Monster against the chalkboard with her telekinetic powers, is also reminiscent of a panel from the original 1980 comic. It's just one of a number of nods in the direction of geek culture that would appeal to fans of the show, but it also provides some clues as to what might happen to Eleven in future seasons. As anyone who has read the original comic will know, Jean Grey doesn't stay dead for long. So like the Phoenix from which her alter-ego takes its name, we can all expect Eleven to rise from the ashes of her apparent demise.

YOUTUBE

After the success of his breakout role as Will Byers on *Stranger Things*, Noah Schnapp launched his own YouTube channel. Entitled Schnapptube, the channel has more than 8,000 subscribers who tune in to watch the actor's semi-regular blogs about his life.

ZITS

American television typically serves up teenagers who represent aspirational adolescence, a rose-tinted view of teenage years, as beautiful young people do amazing things. However, unless you grew up in *The O.C.* or *Beverly Hills 90210* the reality for most is somewhat different. You didn't drive expensive cars or wear designer clothing, and you probably didn't have immaculate hair, skin, and make-up every time you left the house either.

It's this kind of authenticity that the Duffer Brothers tried to capture in *Stranger Things*. After all, the coiffured figure of Steve aside, these characters are not the cool kids. They are not cheerleaders, quarterbacks, or leather jacket-clad bad boys. They are geeks – the kind of kids who excel at science, play Dungeons & Dragons, or enjoy other eclectic interests like photography and British punk rock.

Perhaps no-one embodies that authenticity more than Barb, who became a cult figure even after her demise during *Stranger Things*' first season. After all Barb isn't just the kind of girl you'd expect to see in a real life school; she's the kind of girl you probably went to school with.

During an interview with NPR in 2016 the Duffer Brothers spoke about how they wanted their teenagers to be as realistic as possible. 'Our teens have like acne ... I'm glad we didn't, you know, cover it up,' Ross Duffer said. 'Nowadays you can digitally fix all those flaws. But to me it's important to try to keep that and make it feel as real as possible.'